# THE
# BIG
# IDEA

## 52 WAYS TO BE A BETTER LEADER NOW

Published by
AKA-Publishing
Columbia, Missouri

ISBN 978-1-942168-60-7

# THE
# **BIG**
# IDEA

## 52 WAYS TO BE A BETTER LEADER NOW

### TONY RICHARDS
Founder and CEO,
Clear Vision Development

This book is dedicated to my wife Ann Marie, for the tireless and constant support throughout our wonderful years together. Without you, this book would not be possible. Thank you for choosing me; I love you.

To my parents, Dickie and Shirley, without you, I would not be here. You provided the foundation for the person I am today.

To my two loyal and loving blue heeler dogs, Oreo and Davey. I just want to be the person you think I am.

# Introduction

I grew up in Lola, a small rural farming community in Western Kentucky. The total length of Lola when it was a thriving little community was hardly even a mile long in any direction. In the sphere of this small town, both of my grandparents were entrepreneurs in their own businesses. On one side of town, my grandfather on my dad's side of the family, owned & operated a Purina brand feed store. On the opposite side of town, my grandfather on my mom's side of the family, owned & operated a Texaco service station. My dad's passion, since he came into this world, did not revolve around either of these types of businesses; but rather in the ownership and training of Quarter Horses, especially emphasizing cutting routines with livestock. My own passion was sports, particularly baseball, which I began playing at around six years old.

Sometime around the age of ten or eleven, I saw an episode of the old television show *The Outer Limits*. In this particular episode, Cliff Robertson owned a radio station and increased the power to the point he was able to contact other planets. I thought this was incredibly cool. Also around this time, I saw two movies, which fueled my passion for broadcasting. One was *American Graffiti*. During the entire movie, Wolfman Jack was announcing on the radio in the background over various songs from the early 60s. Eventually in the movie, Richard Dreyfuss tracks down and encounters Wolfman Jack at the radio station on the outskirts of town. Bam, I thought. I love this. The other movie was Clint Eastwood's *Play Misty For Me*. In the movie, Clint plays a radio announcer who gets himself in trouble when Jessica Walter develops an obsession for him. All three of these productions caused me to get the broadcasting bug. I started working at the local radio station in Marion, Kentucky when I was fifteen in 1978 on Sunday mornings. I continued to develop my broadcasting career through school until I landed a management position in 1983. I worked my way up the ranks to get a major management position in 1985.

Sometime in 1986, I started experiencing something I call "career salvation." I had a connection with a fellow named Charlie Mifflin. Charlie was a semi-retired chemicals executive who had been very successful. Charlie came to help run a company with me in 1986. I was failing pretty badly. Mainly because I was in over my head and I didn't really know what I was doing. I was long on youthful exuberance and horribly short on real work business experience. I had studied the industry I was in a great deal for the previous ten years or so. But with the exception of my experience in our family business, I had not spent much time on business fundamentals. Charlie was awesome. He started identifying my strengths and weaknesses as a leader. He started teaching me about business and financials. He started teaching me about negotiation. He was giving me a real world MBA.

This had a profound effect on me. I started thinking about the many others out in the world like me. Folks who had plenty of opportunity but not enough hands-on work experience. Charlie's wonderful and valuable help to me as a young executive is what eventually led me to become a consultant myself. I know the real struggles managers can have in a complex business world in which they feel totally alone. Who do you talk to that you can trust? You are careful when you to talk to your bosses, because you don't want them to lose confidence in you. You have to be selective in who you talk to in your reporting line because you want them to believe you know what you are doing and you don't want to appear clueless or weak. Consultants and coaches like myself provide leaders with that confidante you can trust. Someone who can provide the advice and guidance without being emotionally connected to your organization or your work.

One of the things I did during the time spent with Charlie was to develop a zealous journaling habit. I wrote down everything. I wrote as I was learning. I also developed a zealous reading habit. I wrote down everything I read that was significant. I purchased audiotapes and videotapes of experts teaching various subjects. I journaled it all. Everything I experienced on the job, I recorded in my journal. I wrote down what I was thinking and what I was feeling. Today, I still have all those journals and I still like to go back and read some of the things I wrote down thirty-some years ago. There are many, many things I would have forgotten had I not written them down. There are things even today that I publish on my blog or in published articles that I actually wrote many years ago that have never been public. As time progressed, writing became a passion for me. In 2004, when we started our consulting business, I started blogging and have written something new at least once a week since then. Often, I write something new every day.

In late 2012, I started writing what I called "Big Idea Memos" centered around—yep, you guessed it—Big Ideas. Generally, I would write the memo blog posts on a Sunday morning to have them posted on our website the next Monday morning and then we would email them to our clients and subscribers the Monday following in a newsletter. My thoughts at the time were to sit down and write about something I believed would be on the minds of executives, managers and entrepreneurs. Something, which either had occurred, was occurring, or would occur sometime in the future. Each time I would write one of the Big Idea posts, I would envision a person sitting and reading it and being thankful someone either had been through a similar issue or was thinking of ways to at least provide some advice or direction.

This book is laid out in a fashion in which the Big Idea memos are organized into sections that correspond with my Galaxy of You model. The Sun is power and is the primary energy source your entire galaxy revolves around. In the Galaxy of You, the same is true. You are at the center, providing the energy and power for the entirety of your life. That is why when you improve or get better, everything in your sphere of influence or galaxy improves or gets better. As you expand your knowledge and talents, you expand yourself, which expands your Galaxy of You.

**Section One is all about leading yourself.**

I picked some of my favorite Big Idea Memos, which have to do with personal and professional development. The subject matter here covers everything from finding your purpose, vision, managing pain, goal setting, doing the work of leadership, to spiritual matters. You can't possibly begin leading others or leading your organization until you have spent some time working on leading yourself.

**Section Two focuses on leading others.**

**Section Three is about leading your organization.**

**Section Four is about leading in your community.**

The book is structured so you can use it as a weekly self-improvement session or at your own pace. Some of the points you may need less than a week to work on while other may need more time. Each Big Idea comes with suggested focus points and action steps for you to think about and implement. I am sure you know developing yourself, especially if there is change involved, is more of a process than an event. Just reading a book is not enough; you have to put action with your learning. My philosophy in developing leaders has always been to follow a very concentrated three-step process. Explanation-Demonstration-Practice. So, in each memo, I put forth an effort to explain in a couple of paragraphs the concept of the memo, then demonstrate the concept in the focus point and give you something to practice in the action step.

It is my most sincere desire for this book to be a very beneficial and powerful tool for you to develop more of the endless potential you have as a leader. I have found that the majority of people are at their most fulfilled stage in life when they are operating as excellent performers while creating limitless value for themselves and their organizations.

That is my wish and hope for you.

# Foreword

Do you want to get better?

Who doesn't, right? But why do many people struggle with self-improvement? It could be your work life, personal life, relationships, etc. Tony Richards can help you transform your life towards the person you want to be. But like anything else, you'd better want it badly enough, listen and make changes. You see, I should know, as Tony has not only helped me personally, but he's helped our company transform into a powerhouse organization. We've improved our profitability dramatically by implementing enormous change. We've made thirty-one acquisitions in three years and are growing the company to record heights.

How did we do it? We listened to Tony and his message. Listened and eventually rolled up our sleeves and got to work. We've been using Tony's guidance to help us face our brutal facts and to come up with positive solutions. We've taken Tony's advice and addressed all those issues that had been holding us back for so long. As you know change is very difficult. Tony first helped me understand my limitations as a leader, and then we worked on the company. Not only did our sales unit volumes set records, but our margins did as well! We went from losing money to profitability of $28 million in one year! Did we have challenges? No doubt! But Tony's message resonated with me and my people, and so well that all it took was to understand that we were our own worst enemy and soon we began fixing it.

I realize our improved results sound simple, and in fact it was simple. But simple doesn't mean it was easy! Our team had to realize we could in fact make the positive changes we needed to make in order for the company to succeed. Much of our challenge was simply getting our people to believe how good we could be. We used metrics to measure our key performance indicators. Our people gained alignment and began to understand that in order for us to reach our vision of a great company, change needed to be our best friend. Tony's message was spot-on for us.

As I look back on my thirty-year career and the many challenges I've had, the majority of the solutions were to simply step up my leadership and take accountability for myself. I believe most of the time we know and understand the changes that need to be made in order to make progress, but for whatever reason we rationalize and procrastinate. For me it was gaining a better understanding of the talent and eventually making changes in my staff. For you it might be something else. We used real-life stories to prove our points. Whatever issues you or your company face, Tony's book provides excellent solutions for you to pursue. Tony breaks the book down into four major categories: Leading Yourself, Leading Others, Leading Your Organization, and Leading Your Community. The book follows a perfect progression, as you can't lead anyone else until you lead yourself.

Enjoy this wonderful book!

Mark Fenner
CEO, MFA Oil Company

## Section 1: Leading Yourself

THE
**BIG**
IDEA

BIG IDEA #**1**

# Finding Your Life Purpose

**Most everyone feels a pull toward some defining purpose in his or her life.** We spot intermittent clues along the way that make the pull more apparent. There is always some form of evolution, or at least some movement toward an overall defining life purpose. On the other hand, we become so distracted with the day-to-day tasks, activities, or goals that these feelings must be shelved or ignored in order for us to get back to our busy lives.

We sometimes put ourselves in line for consequences because we don't identify our over-arching life purpose. One of these consequences comes when our inner-self knows we are out of sync with our outer behavior. This causes some frustration and quite a bit of dissatisfaction; things seem a bit hollow. It may feel like a lack of inner peace or confidence has been instilled in your life.

When you are on the verge of discovering your purpose, it often feels like an inclination that continues to push you. Sometimes this discovery is right in front of your eyes, but you don't allow yourself to see it.

## FOCUS POINT

Discovering your life purpose means letting go of self-interest. When you're highly focused on yourself or meeting your goals in your work, life, and relationships, your purpose becomes obscure. Your ego covers it like clouds blocking the sun. Ego is part of being human, but you must be aware of it and keep it in check. Letting go can help you find your deepest purpose.

## ACTION STEP

Create a Purpose Statement for your life. Many people don't understand their purpose or what they are meant to be doing until very late in their lives. Unfortunately, some never find it. It's important to explore this part of your life to avoid regret later. There is a huge advantage in being at peace with yourself and understanding why you are on this planet at this particular time. Know that you have a strong contribution to make regarding others. Once you have this confidence, the pursuit of your vision becomes easier and a lot more enjoyable.

Here are some exercises you can do to help give you a clear vision:
• Journal and dedicate a few blank pages to this section
• Schedule some quiet time
• Clear your mind

Contemplate some of these questions:

1. What makes you smile?
   (Activities, people, events, hobbies, projects, etc.)
2. What are your favorite things to do?
3. What activities make you lose track of time?

4. What makes you feel great about yourself?
5. Who inspires you most?
   *(Family, friends, authors, artists, leaders, etc.)*
6. Which qualities inspire you in each person?
7. What are you naturally good at?
   *(Skills, abilities, gifts, etc.)*
8. What do people typically ask you for help with?
9. If you had to teach something, what would you teach?
10. What would you regret not fully doing, being, or having in your life?
11. What are the challenges, difficulties, and hardships you've overcome or are in the process of overcoming? How did you do it?
12. What causes do you strongly connect with?
13. How can you use your talents, passions, and values as resources to serve, help, and contribute?

Once you have answered the questions in your journal, try putting it together in a few paragraphs you can mold into your Purpose Statement for your life. This can be a powerful guiding star for your own self-direction.

# #2 BIG IDEA
## What Success Means to You

**Many people want success, and it can be defined in many different ways.** Some define success as enjoying a comfortable lifestyle, some as getting a strong work/life balance, while others define it as simply providing for family. How you define success has an important impact on how you make decisions on a daily basis.

When you think about it, success is not really something to be pursued. It is actually attracted to you through becoming the person you are to be.

One of the things I have learned in my life is that success doesn't come through achieving a singular goal, such as attaining a certain amount of money or reaching a particular number on the scale. True success is the transformation that happens when you are in pursuit of the goal. Money won't stay forever, but the true transformation in you will.

### FOCUS POINT

Three important points about success:

#1: It's important that you do not allow the crowd to define success for you. You define success for you.

#2: Success is not restricted—it's open to anyone with the courage to dream and then act on those dreams.

4

#3: Sometimes people feel frustrated because they cannot see the connection between what they are doing every day and the larger picture of success. It's important to realize success is being on the road to achieving your dreams.

Be thankful you are on the road; things tend to change and become clearer as you travel. People who sit still always have the same view.

## ACTION STEP

Take some time to write down your definition of success. Don't spend more than five minutes on this. Write it in your journal, don't self-edit the first time, and just let it flow. You can always go back and change it later. Once you have it down, take some time to reflect on your life and how you are on the road traveling toward what you've written. Meditate on that thought. Feel free to add to your definition as new thoughts come to you.

# #3 BIG IDEA
## Preventing a Shortsighted Vision

**Where are the edges? The life you see for yourself currently is not necessarily the life of your future.** The business you see for yourself currently is not necessarily the business of your future. The career you see for yourself at this moment is not necessarily the career of your future. We all view these things through our own viewpoints or paradigms. There are edges or sides on our frame of reference; sometimes we call it our box. The edges are made up of our fears, limitations, and false assumptions. Most people sincerely believe that their own limits are also the limits of the world. Fortunately, our limits are not the world's limits—they are simply our world's limits.

There was a time when it was believed that no human being could run a mile in less than four minutes. In fact, the thought was that anyone who did accomplish it would die soon afterwards. Roger Bannister broke this paradigm on May 6, 1954 by running a mile in 3 minutes and 59.4 seconds. After that, an interesting thing happened—another human being broke his record after only forty-six days. Once Bannister broke through the limit, several others started accomplishing what was previously believed impossible.

6

## FOCUS POINT

We see the world not as it is, but as we are. Once you begin to think about yourself and your perceived limitations from a different perspective, you begin to think outside your box. After that thinking, a whole new set of possibilities begins to present itself.

What limitations have you bought into for your vision? Your thoughts create your reality. If you believe something is not possible, you will never take the action necessary to make it a reality. Therefore, your vision will be shortsighted and limited. Your perception will become your reality.

## ACTION STEP

Re-examine your path forward. What false assumptions are you making in terms of what you cannot have, do, and be? Leaders think in terms of the future, return to the present, and then proceed forward with action to create what they have seen. No one can see your vision as clearly as you; don't expect other people to immediately validate your thinking. Think Roger Bannister or Christopher Columbus—almost no one believed they would succeed, but they did.

# #4 BIG IDEA
## Goal Setting for Success

**New beginnings. The start of the year is a natural time to try to integrate your past, present, and future.** Of course, you don't have to wait for the new year to make a new beginning. It is important to use these three time frames in a way that fills you with confidence and excitement, instead of stressing you out. This means goal-setting is risky business. If failures start accumulating, you begin to doubt whether you can reach goals. This may result in giving up altogether. We like some flexibility in our lives, but research suggests that being as specific as possible is a lot more effective in goal-setting. Putting forth specific pieces checked off in strict order seems harder at the start, but it actually leads to greater accomplishment than a vague, ambiguous plan.

The problem with resolutions is that they tend to get the timeframes all wrong. They're about trying to fix something from your past. Shifting your thinking can help. Look back over the past year and celebrate your progress. How far did you progress forward? Why is this a win? We often forget to acknowledge our wins, but this celebration fills you up with morale. This thinking turns your past, present, and future into useful tools, rather than another "stick" to punish yourself with. The "stick" method is discouraging and guilt-inducing, and it doesn't work. Ask anyone who has routinely set New Year's resolutions, only to have them all broken by Valentine's Day. Resolutions are not as powerful as goals. Goals, when set right, include a mechanism of accountability and measurement that moves you toward some desirable outcome. You gain power and accelerate your progress when you strive for something positive, rather than trying to avoid that thing you don't want to happen (again).

## FOCUS POINT

Setting SMART goals. What others have accomplished, you can also accomplish—by learning my five must-know SMART goals, and by developing key habits of execution. This involves setting SMART goals and getting as much information as possible on what you want to accomplish. Once you learn and practice the SMART goal-setting process, you too will accomplish business success and develop the habits to push you forward. SMART is an acronym for the five steps of specific, measurable, action-oriented, realistic, and time-specific goals. It is one of the most effective tools used by high achievers to reach their business goals consistently.

The SMART model of goal setting:

S = Specific
M = Measurable
A = Action-Oriented
R = Realistic
T = Time-Specific

Once your business goals are SMART, break down each goal into specific, clear tasks and activities needed to accomplish the goals. It's important to periodically review your goals and make adjustments if necessary.

## ACTION STEP

Set goals and share. Once you use the formula to set three to five goals for yourself, you will want to share them. Research shows that writing down your goals, sharing them with friends, and sending regular updates about your progress can boost your chances of success. This is why hiring a coach is effective for so many leaders. Leaders who wrote their goals down and shared their progress succeeded about 75% of the time.

## BIG IDEA #5
# The Work of Leadership

**It isn't always what you think. Leadership has nothing to do with the title on your business card or the size of your office.** Leadership is a philosophy of how you conduct yourself. Leading is a state of mind, in which you make yourself and others better, hoping to improve every situation. Leaders hate the status quo; they are willing to maintain focus and work hard to build something better.

Developing your leadership ability for personal and professional success takes a lot of work. Usually when we look at the best, they make it look so easy. The reality is the backstory of what they did to get to the best level. We always become fascinated with the event, rather than the process, but the process is what makes the event so amazing.

### FOCUS POINT

Search your intentions about being a leader. What are you willing to do to be the leader you are destined to be? Does this mean giving up your fear of something? Does it mean giving up your need to be right? Does it mean giving up your need to have everything perfect? What are you willing to do today? If you are a leader, then you will be called upon to do the work of leadership.

11

## ACTION STEP

Identify what you need to work on. Make a complete list of everything that is holding you back from being the leader you know you are supposed to be. Pick one entry from the list you know you can work on, and take action. Be totally honest with yourself, and most importantly, pick something you know you will follow through on. It is so important to keep our commitments to ourselves!

BIG IDEA #6

# The Processing of Pain

**Growing pains. It's been proven that when we grow and develop ourselves in order to gain strength, pain is part of the process.** Pain has been given to us to signal that we are approaching a limitation of some kind. Simultaneously, we are hard-wired in such a way that the process of growing ourselves requires us to push our limits. Personal and professional growth is the result of adapting to the barriers we encounter. When we hit that pain line, we are at an important place in our decision-making process: Do we push forward into the uncomfortable, unknown areas we are encountering? Or, will we drop back into the safety of our familiar comfort zone?

We are programmed to stop, fight, or flee. Most of our lives, we have been taught to alleviate pain as soon as possible. Our brains have been taught that pain is a danger signal, and we need to stop it or cover it up as soon as possible. Our fight or flight reactions kick in; we lash out at the pain and those involved, or we get away from it as quickly as possible. When we encounter this in our professional lives, as far as growth opportunities are concerned, we find ways to discredit or avoid it. We find ways around our barriers when we encounter them, and as a result we make little to no progress.

## FOCUS POINT

Become comfortable being uncomfortable. Many leaders respond well to these growing pains. They understand what is causing them, and they have learned that if they proactively deal with their obstacles, they can learn more and become more experienced. Most learning comes from making mistakes and being uncomfortable. If you can train yourself to stay in the uncomfortable zone, to think and to reflect rather than fight or flee, it can lead to faster growth. The processing of pain is the first major decision you make toward stronger growth.

## ACTION STEP

Think about it. What is your tendency when the going gets tough? Do you fight against it, run away from it, or reflect deeply about it? Do you allow the pain of being uncomfortable to stand in the way of your progress? Do you understand how to manage your growth pains to produce progress?

## BIG IDEA #7
## Expanding Your Limits

**What do you believe? One of our most underestimated professional development tools is the power our beliefs have over our level of productivity and success.** A belief is something that we have placed high trust and confidence in. Our beliefs shape our perception of the world around us and help us to decide what ideas and concepts we accept as true and valid. These beliefs are things we have decided to think are true based on information we have received up to this point in our lives. In other words, as we proceed from our youngest point to the current state, we realize certain assumptions we have made in our lives might not have been as accurate as our current viewpoint of the world.

With this thought in mind, it is apparent that many of us have beliefs that limit our success. They might be beliefs about ourselves, our talents, what it takes to be a success, or how we should relate to people. If you study history, you will find that beliefs have continued to evolve and change throughout human existence. We have learned in school that people once believed the world was flat! Moving beyond your limiting beliefs is a critical step toward breaking barriers.

The important thing to remember is that you have placed beliefs there, and you can remove them. Every human is capable of amazing things, and has unlimited potential. As an example of the power of beliefs, how you perceive and process that last statement will determine how much you can grow.

## FOCUS POINT

Our subconscious mind does not argue with our conscious mind. Whatever your conscious mind decides is true, your subconscious mind accepts as fact or belief. Your subconscious then goes to work to differentiate things you have decided against and what you believe is true. If your conscious mind decides you can only achieve a certain level of promotion, your subconscious works hard to make sure it happens. If your conscious mind decides it's possible you will run the company one day, your subconscious will go to work looking for the opportunities to make it happen.

## ACTION STEP

Overcome beliefs that limit you. Since you own it, you can do with it what you will. You can hang on to it, or you can remove it. The first step is to recognize it and realize how it limits you. Next, decide if you want to keep it or discard it. Create an opposite statement of belief to counteract and give yourself permission to be, act, or feel the new way. Practice daily! (Example: "I believe I won't advance in the company because I am a woman." Give yourself permission to believe: "I will be promoted because I am good at what I do. I am a go-getter.")

BIG IDEA #8

# Stress & Healthy Pressure

**Stress affects every human being. Stress has become an American epidemic.** If you are over forty, you probably don't have memories of walking up to your parents when something was wrong, and they said, "I'm stressed out!" It's become a more common response as we've uncovered more knowledge about stress. The majority of leaders today have an abundance of stress in their lives, and based on reports, it appears to be rising. According to the American Institute of Stress, 70 to 90% of all visits to a primary physician's office are stress-related.

Too much stress is deadly, but healthy pressure can make you a champion leader. Even though stress has been identified as one of the most pressing problems for leaders, it is manageable. One way of managing it involves learning the difference between stress and healthy pressure. Stress is deadly for you in all kinds of health-related ways. Healthy pressure can spur you to greatness. Stress is not caused by the exterior event; it is your reaction to the exterior event. Healthy pressure can get you out of bed in the morning and raise your energy level when you need to get something important accomplished.

## FOCUS POINT

Your job is to notice challenging situations you find yourself facing. What is your reaction or response? You react when you have an emotional moment, which feels like stress. You respond when you are decisive or move in a productive fashion. Raise your level of self-awareness by making notes of how various situations affect you, and whether you are reacting or responding.

## ACTION STEP

Make a list with a few columns:

Which situations caused you to become emotional and frazzled? Has your heart rate increased?

You may have become vocal, or perhaps really introverted. Make notes of the event and how you reacted.

Also, which events did you respond to that seemed like healthy pressure?

Note how you responded to those events. Develop an awareness of the signals that key you to each behavior. This way you can make better decisions regarding that behavior, and dramatically reduce stress in your life and leadership role.

## BIG IDEA #9
## Make Change
## Your Best Friend

**We are really lucky. Human beings are the only living creatures on the planet equipped with the awesome power of change.** I am sitting in my workspace, looking toward the wooded area behind my home at some squirrels playfully running across limbs and jumping from tree to tree. They cannot change their environment. They are pre-programmed with instincts to respond to changes in their environment, but they cannot create the changes. If for some reason their ecosystem is disrupted, they are virtually powerless to change it. I, on the other hand, am sitting in a comfortable space in an environment totally controlled by me. I can adjust the temperature and the lighting. I can turn on music if I so desire. I can also change rooms, or even areas of the country or world if I so choose to facilitate that change.

Sometimes we are stubborn, sometimes afraid. We sometimes want to resist change, and other times we are paralyzed by our fears. We should consider proceeding similarly to the circus high-wire walker, teetering this way and that way. In times of turbulent change, we make slight corrections, but keep going across the wire until we feel the steady, solid platform of the new normal at the opposite end. The important thing is to stay the course—make adjustments, but keep transforming into something productive and powerful.

# FOCUS POINT

Opportunities come to those who are prepared. This is true for both leaders and organizations. Organizations follow leaders, and unfortunately, many leaders focus on what is happening now rather than the change the future holds. The future belongs to those who create and master it. If things are not going as intended, how long will it be before you facilitate a change in direction?

If you are not making progress on a goal, change the action steps or your rate of execution on the current steps. Change something! Make sure you don't confuse activity with progress and accomplishment. Reflect on the progress, not the time and effort. Make change your best friend, and adjust accordingly.

# ACTION STEP

Contemplate three areas of change:

1.  Embrace Change: You can either go with it or fight it. If you fight it, you will lose. What will be the consequences of going with it?

2.  Promote Change: Stop being so self-focused. We usually like change better if it is our idea. Don't just get on board with your own ideas; help someone promote theirs.

3.  Lead Change: Things are moving faster than ever. The rate of change is always accelerating; you have less time to adjust, so why not be out in front for a change?

# BIG IDEA #10
## Cultivating a Positive Outlook

**Leaders must take note of things which need improvement, and they must make the decision to look for the positive in every situation.** I often present a concept at workshops called "Roll With It/Improve It." In short, the concept is, if something is outside of our control, we must decide to roll with it. If it is something we can control, or at the very least influence, then we can decide whether or not to improve it.

One of the few things we have complete control over is ourselves. We have control over the way we choose to behave, and how we view things. Along these lines, the amount of self-awareness we have increases our competency. When we are faced with adversity, we can choose to focus on the negative in the situation, or we can choose to look for the good and the positive.

Changing your viewpoint from negative to positive is something everyone can do with a little coaching and practice. When leaders embrace this practice, the benefits are beyond amazing. Many of my clients say this practice is one of the top five reasons for increased results and success. After adopting this practice, some clients still don't realize the effect viewpoint has on their life and leadership. However, they comment that their amount of "good luck" has dramatically increased, and their "bad luck" has decreased. Changing from a negative viewpoint to a positive one does tend to have a snowball effect. Unfortunately, it also works in the reverse.

## FOCUS POINT

Start to really become aware of your attitude and viewpoint regarding every situation in your life. Which ones do you automatically place in the negative, and which get placed as positive? It's important to be cognizant that how you view situations in your own life might also be the way you view them in the lives of others. As a leader, it is your responsibility to add as much value as you can to the people you lead.

## ACTION STEP

Write down all the negative events surrounding your life right now. (This can also include your professional life.) Write the name of the negative event at the top of each page, then list all the positives you can think of that come from this event. See if you can fill the page. Remember, the objective is to begin to change your viewpoint; it may take a few of these exercises to see results. You also must have the sincere intention to become more positive.

Get out of your own way!

BIG IDEA #

# BIG IDEA #11
## Other People's Thoughts Are None of Your Business

**Have you ever wondered why we don't have the ability to read other people's minds?** It's because thoughts are private. Every person has the ability to think as they wish. Your thoughts are one thing that can never be taken away from you. At the same time, one of the things that can cripple leaders is oversensitivity to what people think of us.

You want the truth? Here it is:

The truth is, no matter how hard you may try to gain approval, you will never meet every person's expectations. There will always be someone who does not approve. There will always be someone who does not agree with you. No matter how hard you try or how well you perform, someone, somewhere will be critical of your performance. The sooner you accept this fact, the better your performance will be.

Let me tell you what I am NOT saying.

I am not saying we should ignore the feelings, thoughts, needs, or opinions of other people. You should take note of what others are communicating. What I am saying is, if you are not careful, you will end up being mediocre if you are trying to satisfy everyone all the time. If you try to please everyone, you will satisfy nobody…especially yourself.

If your intention is to do the very best you can, you should be good with it. If you believe at the end of each day that you have performed at your very best level, you should be happy with it.

## FOCUS POINT

If you obsess over your feedback, whether good or bad, you will be tortured. No matter how good you are, someone will rate you average or poor. No matter how bad you are, someone will give you a good rating. You will be the human roller-coaster leader if you live your life based on the feedback and opinions of others. The best attitude is to NOT take things personally; no matter what happens around you in regards to feedback.

## ACTION STEP

Examine your performance closely for examples of trying to be popular rather than effective. Leadership requires self-confidence in order to maintain a healthy detachment from the opinions of others. This is important for the leader who should say NO when they are pressured to say YES. Remember, being a reliable and consistent leader is more important than being popular for the short-term.

BIG IDEA #**12**

# Your Head & Your Heart Can Provide Competing Commitments

**Our hearts and our minds are separate entities, and they perform separate functions.** When I talk about our hearts, I'm not talking about the organ which pumps blood throughout our body. I'm referencing our emotional center, the place where our emotions sit and from which they emanate. When I refer to our minds, I'm not talking about our physical brains. I'm talking about where our logic and thinking reside.

Both of these components provide valuable functions. Our hearts provide our get-up-and-go; our emotions and passion are fuel to the fire that drives us onward. Our logic and thinking help us to plan and make sense of the world around us. Sometimes, these two functions are not in harmony. This causes conflict, and we often have to make a tough decision: Do I go with my heart or my head? Since they are YOUR heart and head, you are committed to both; I call this competing commitments.

Your head is telling you to stay in your job, but your heart is telling you to start a new business. Your head is telling you to invest, but your heart is telling you to buy what you want in this moment. This is competing commitment. The decisions you make in these situations are going to control the results you have in the future.

## FOCUS POINT

You should focus on how each of these components works where you are concerned. I know this sounds simple, and it is. Your head is for thinking and your heart is for feeling, not the other way around. Many people rely on one or the other too much; they may not ever be in touch with the opposite one. For instance, in workshops, I have asked certain participants how they are feeling in the moment, and the response has been, "I don't know." However, they did know the opposite answer: "What are you thinking?"

## ACTION STEP

Start paying attention to each of these components, both your heart and your head. Which one is more dominant? See if you can "put one on hold" and listen to the other one. Also, see if you can synchronize them and get them on the same page. Try to use your heart to summon passion and drive, while using your head to visualize the possible result of an option.

# The Morning Routine

**How you start your day will largely determine the course of your day.** Getting up in the morning is more than just winning the battle with the bed. Getting your day started in a proactive and purposeful way can make a huge difference in the trajectory of your day. Every leader is looking for wins throughout the day, every day. Getting up early is your first win of the day! It gives you a huge psychological advantage. Most people in the world won't do it; they will prefer to sleep in. Research has shown consistently that successful people get up early. In many cases, CEOs who run global companies get used to getting up early, because they have regular calls with managers in so many time zones. A CEO in the United States has to get up early to have a wrap-up call with his driving force manager in Asia.

Most of Apple's employees know the majority of email communication they get from CEO Tim Cook is going to come between 4:30 and 5:00 AM. Cook is typically in the gym by five in the morning. Disney CEO Robert Iger spends what he calls "quiet time" between 4:30 and 6:00 AM every morning. The youngest CEO in the NBA, Brett Yormark of the New Jersey Nets, says he gets up at 3:30 AM, and is in the office by 4:30. He sleeps in on weekends, getting up at 7:00 AM. Avon Products CEO Andrea Jung gets up at 5:00 AM, heads to the gym, and is at her deal going full steam at 8:00 AM. Why are so many successful people early risers?

They have found that starting your engine so early in the morning, while others are not, is a huge advantage. It gives you more time than other people. It gives you time that is uninterrupted, when distractions are at a bare minimum. You can be more proactive and less reactive. The reasons why this works are countless.

## FOCUS POINT

Get an early start. I have personally been an early riser for years. Growing up in an agricultural community, getting up early is a way of life. I am so fortunate that getting up early was instilled in me early-on as a habit. When school was not in session during the summer months, we had to have the animals all fed and the feed store opened by 7:00. My grandfather was a stickler for that. We were not opening by 7:00; we were open at 7:00. I get up around 4:30 every morning, including weekends. I have my morning routine down to a science. You will have to play with yours and adjust for maximum productivity.

## ACTION STEPS

Make out your Big 5 list for the day—what gets scheduled, gets done. Do some prayer or meditation or breathing exercises to make the transition from sleeping to awake. Have quiet time to think; often your brain is the most active right before you wake up. Do some visualization of your day and your future. Exercise! Go to the gym, walk your dog, or write in your journal.

# BIG IDEA #14
## The Spiritual Side of Leadership

**We are unique. I understand that when you begin to talk the spiritual side of things, you can introduce an argument almost anywhere.** It comes down to simply what you believe. My beliefs tell me that humans are much different than any other living thing on Earth. We are not animals, plants, minerals, chemicals, or substances; although we have some of these things and share similarities with others. Some people believe we are an extension of these things, or just a more advanced form through the process of evolution. I don't believe this. I believe human beings are unique, and we stand in our own category of living thing.

I listened to a speech given recently by someone who said there are no natural resources on Earth except one. He believed the only natural resource on Earth is human beings. The reason is because all resources of the Earth have been present for all of its history, but many of them were not utilized or valuable until human beings made them useful or valuable. Take oil for example. Oil was a resource of the Earth for a long time, but until humans developed the need for energy, light, and fuel, oil was a worthless resource. This speaks to the spiritual side of us as leaders.

Our spirituality comes from being created uniquely—to be creative, and to be in charge. We were put in charge of this

29

planet to cultivate it and make it useful and productive. As leaders, that is our job. Our responsibilities are to produce quality environments, products, services, and outcomes. We were not created to just consume, but more importantly, to produce.

## FOCUS POINT

Becoming authentic. The spiritual side of leadership is important because, by developing your spiritual side, you begin to realize your true self—then you start to become more authentic. Each human being has been designed to fulfill their purpose. That purpose guides the focus of your life, and enables you to accomplish what you were born to accomplish.

However you develop your spiritual side is up to you. However, I strongly encourage you to develop it. I continue to find my spiritual development through the Bible. Whatever you have to read and assimilate to develop in that area of your life, I strongly suggest you do it as soon and as often as possible.

## ACTION STEP

Read something to develop your spirituality daily. There are many devotional books out there that give you short reads and action steps you can easily adapt into your morning routine.

## BIG IDEA #15
# You Are Becoming What You Think About

**Your actions are directly linked to your thoughts.** Everything starts with thinking. You become and act out what you think. The thoughts you generate, nurture, and entertain become self-fulfilling prophecies. Your thoughts shape your expectations. If you expect your life to be extraordinary, it will. Conversely, if you don't expect your life to be extraordinary, it won't.

Actions equal results over time. The actions you take each day create the results in your life. Those actions are in direct connection to your thoughts. Every action has been preceded by a thought. Your thoughts and perceptions drive your reality. A human being will never act bigger than their thoughts. Dream big, and big behavior will follow. Think small = play small.

"You will never go higher than your thinking."
— British Prime Minister Benjamin Disraeli

### FOCUS POINT

Get inspiration from those you admire who you believe broke out of their limitations, realistic or otherwise. Reading and/or watching biographies will help you do this. Since this concept has such cascading power throughout every dimension of our lives, we really need to consider and focus on it. Also, since

31

thought is limitless, why create mental limits? The answer is not: "I'm just trying to be realistic." Of course, being realistic should be part of your goal-setting process, but where would our world be without people who transcend the impossible?

## ACTION STEP

Make a conscious effort to capture your thoughts by journaling about them. Remember, only the average person has average thoughts. Write down the amount of money you would like to make, or that you would like your business to be generating. Write down places you would like to visit. Write down people or organizations you want to be involved with helping.

Grow your thoughts, grow your life.

THE
**BIG**
IDEA

## BIG IDEA #16
## Getting Focused is Easy

**Rabbit-Focused Wisdom. My grandmother used to always tell me you can't chase two rabbits; you will lose both of them.** Think about that. Have you been having a hard time with your career, your team, or your business? What rabbits have you been chasing? Perhaps you allowed an unexpected phone call to take you on a side-trip that wasted ten minutes, and got you no further progress toward your main goal for the day. Many people think they work hard because they have lots of activities, but very few of these activities are ones that generate revenue.

Getting focused is not the hard part. Getting focused is easy. Staying focused is hard. Why? It's because we react rather than respond. There are so many rabbits screaming for our attention and prompting us to react. Reaction happens almost automatically; it's like someone or something pushing your buttons. Responding is something we do on purpose and mindfully. Reaction is something that happens in a millisecond snap decision. Response is when we decide to make it happen.

### FOCUS POINT

What are all the rabbits you chase? How much time and energy does it cost you? Don't commit to chasing rabbits. It's not what you are willing to do that determines your success; it's what you are not willing to do. What about that tone that sounds as a message appears in the corner of my computer screen to tell me, "You have mail." The problem used to be that I would always stop to see what e-mail just came in. Chasing rabbits. When I turned that e-mail function off, and only paid attention to sending and receiving e-mail at specific times, I was amazed at how much more I was getting done. I simply set times during the day to check and answer e-mail, rather than reacting to that tone, and letting it take me off-task.

## ACTION STEP

Make a list of five key activities that generate the most productivity, and have the biggest pay-off in your job. Your job could be as a manager, a parent, a clerk, a salesperson, or a student. Commit to doing more of those key activities, and less chasing rabbits. Make a list of all the rabbits that cause you to react rather than respond. You might also ask someone who knows you well what things trigger a reaction in you; what causes you to veer off-task and off-focus.

**Winning every battle begins with self-talk.** What is self-talk? Self-talk is the talking you do in your head about the things that happen—your own "running commentary" on your life. Often, this self-talk happens so automatically that you are barely aware of it. What you say to yourself can have a big effect on the way that you feel, and what you can achieve. Most of us are engaged in constant mental chatter—we talk to ourselves all day long, and unfortunately, most of this is negative if not recognized or confronted.

Thoughts = Actions. If we can change the way we think, we can begin to change the actions we take. It is human nature to seek personal growth; whether financially, emotionally, physically, or spiritually. Becoming aware of our self-talk can help us set in motion actions that will bring us greater rewards. Changing self-talk requires some time and practice, since our ways of thinking tend to be quite ingrained.

Personal Story: The first time I learned that my thoughts were powerful, and that they created my reality was a defining moment for me. The subject I am sharing with you has shaped my personal life and my career path for as long as I can recall. It started in sports. When I was on a baseball field or a basketball court, I was dedicated to focusing. I began to notice that as I attempted to focus, I became aware of a dialogue that continued to run through my head. For movie fans, see the Kevin Costner film, *For Love of the Game*. I began to practice not only my physical skills in sports, but the mental aspect as well by using positive self-talk. You can learn to "engage the mechanism."

## FOCUS POINT

You can control the mental aspect of your game (job, career, relationship, etc). You can learn to "unthink" thoughts that do not support what you want to be, do, have, or become. If you cannot stop self-talk, you must replace it. Thinking negative thoughts is not a crime; they simply make it more difficult to live the life you most desire. They are tricky roadblocks you have to navigate around.

On the other hand, positive thoughts are like boosters that propel you toward where you would most like to go. "Engaging the mechanism" by focusing on those positive thoughts and upgrading your self-talk from negative to positive will require you to be more aware of your thoughts. You must also be committed to some practice.

## ACTION STEP

Pay attention to the thoughts you are thinking when you are alone, and when situations come up. If these thoughts are not positive, energizing, and deliberate, replace them with a positive line of thinking. Every person thinks negative thoughts. Do not condemn yourself; you turn a big boat a little at a time. Start off with one day and build yourself up to one week. You may have to verbalize your thoughts. You may need to hear your own voice in order to counter the more silent voice of your mind. Do it. Say it out loud with conviction, purpose, and encouragement. You may want to start your affirmation with, "I deserve…" (love, freedom, happiness, to be positive, etc.).

Create filters. You may need to inventory what is around you. Whatever is around you is feeding your thoughts. Friends, associates, media—they all feed our thinking. Which ones are adding to the positive nature of your self-talk, and which ones are feeding the negative side? Make a list and review it; you might be surprised once you take notice.

# #18 BIG IDEA
# Rate the Power of Your Intentions

**The power of intention.** You may have heard that the road to Hell is paved with good intentions. You may comfort yourself by saying you had good intentions. Rather than thinking of intentions as being good or bad, we should think of them in terms of power level. Intention is not willpower. Intention is the alignment of your conscious and subconscious mind to take action. Think about your intentions being rated on a scale of 1-10. If you had to give each of your intentions a power rating, what score would you give them? The lower the power rating of your intention, the less chance you will take action, and the less chance you will sustain it toward a goal. The higher the power rating of your intention, the higher the chance you will take action again and again, therefore sustaining until reaching the objective.

You have the ability to turn up or down the power of your intentions. Negative thoughts that begin with, "I can't," place you in a victim state. In this state, you automatically are turning down the power of your intention. Did you ever read the children's book, *The Little Engine That Could*? ("I think I can…I think I can…I think I can.") The little engine was simply turning up its power of intention. By doing so it was able to take action and move forward to success.

## FOCUS POINT

How badly do you want it?

Your subconscious is already seeing a picture of the current reality. To achieve your goal, you must combat that image. The best way to do this is to create a new image. If you can't stop thoughts, you must replace them. You want to replace them with ideas that help you turn up the intention to take action toward your desired goals.

## ACTION STEP

Turn up the power. Take a goal you have, and find a way to picture it or touch it consistently. For example, say you want to buy some property. Take weekly walks on the land you want to buy. If you decide to build something there, create drawings of the project and constantly look at them. Actually take time to mentally picture living there. All of these exercises will raise your intent. Take any goal you want to pursue, work on these types of exercises, and turn up the power of your intention until you succeed in achieving the goal.

# #19 BIG IDEA
## The Power of Choice

**Choices have two sides.** Every moment of every day we make choices. Every choice has consequences that contain both costs and benefits. When we open our eyes and minds to the fact that every choice we make changes our experience, it helps clarify our perspective. Some leaders view themselves as responsible for their choices, and some see themselves as powerless victims. A perspective of being responsible means you feel you are the cause of your situation because of the choices you have made. Responsible leaders make things happen. Victim leaders are having things happen to them.

Frankl's Perspective. Viktor Frankl was imprisoned in a Nazi concentration camp during World War II. He saw his parents, his wife, and hundreds of his fellow prisoners die of starvation. Somehow, he survived the camp and chronicled his experiences and viewpoints in his famous work, *Man's Search for Meaning*. Frankl said choice was the driving factor that kept him alive. He said that all human beings have the ability to choose, even in the most undesirable circumstances. He later said that the Statue of Liberty on the East Coast should have a companion Statue of Responsibility on the West Coast to remind us that freedom of choice comes with responsibility and consequences. If we don't make the right choices, we lose our liberty.

## FOCUS POINT

The power of choice gives us the ability to do what we want to do, when we want to do it. You can go where you want, when you want. You also have the ability to be what you want, when you want. Peak performing leaders are in search of choices, solutions, and meaning in life, rather than waiting for random happenings. Remember, there is a cost to everything. Every benefit you experience has a corresponding cost, or something you must give up. You must embrace the notion of choosing the right direction, rather than the easier wrong direction. There are costs for making the right choices, as well as costs for taking the easy way out.

## ACTION STEP

Count the cost. Sometimes we make the wrong choices because the long-term costs are hidden. We don't see the price to pay for smoking, eating wrong, or being in debt. If the cost effect of these decisions was more immediate, we might make different choices. By the same token, sometimes the costs are apparent and the long-term benefits are hidden. For example, when investing for retirement at a young age, think about the choices you are making or have to make coming up, and try to see both the costs and benefits of each choice.

# #20 BIG IDEA
# The Most Committed Always Win

**The definition of commitment doesn't change.**
Commitment means doing what you say you will do. Average leaders believe in this concept when conditions are favorable, or when it's easy to keep their word. Outstanding leaders keep commitments even when it's difficult or it hurts. Outstanding leaders follow through whether it feels good or not. Average leaders do what they feel like, and feelings are subject to change. Commitment should not be subject to change. Outstanding leaders value their word and their principles above anything else. The average leader doesn't care about keeping commitments, and the value of their word becomes cheap. This ranges from customers and co-workers to friends and family; sometimes, even worse, to themselves.

Commitment is the basis for trust. When trust is broken, relationships become unstable. When commitments are not honored, the healthy process of working together becomes shaky and unpredictable. This costs huge amounts of time, emotion, and money, and can destroy health and relationships. Controlling expectations and being solid on what you commit to is the basis to avoid pain. Realize that whatever you say yes to means everything else gets a no. You will have a hard time accomplishing large success without large agreements. Nothing happens without an agreement, and the bigger the better. In a large agreement, anything less than a large commitment, with execution and follow-through, means devastating failure.

## FOCUS POINT

Life and success happen in proportion to the size of promises you make and keep. This works with you and with others. Most people are out of balance on this, as they work hard to keep commitments to others, but often break commitments to themselves with no second thought. Breaking your commitments to yourself can be severely damaging. Your inability to trust yourself will eventually become apparent to those you are asking to trust you.

## ACTION STEP

Don't make excuses. Excuses are a way of breaking your commitments and being dishonest with yourself and others. Average leaders make up excuses when they fear the truth. Average leaders invent seemingly reasonable excuses for everything they fail to accomplish. This helps gain acceptance, approval, and understanding without facing consequences or being honest with themselves and others. This thought should be ingrained in your brain today: The most committed always win; the good guys or the most honorable don't always win. Think about areas where you have made commitment. Where is your commitment on a scale of 1-10? What can you do to strengthen that commitment to carry you to a win?

# Section 2: Leading Others

# BIG IDEA #21
## Your Wealth Is in Your Relationships

**Place a high value on relationships.** However when you measure wealth, you will continually find it in the relationships you develop. If you want to increase your business revenue, it will happen through a trade with someone you have a trusted relationship with. If you want to meet someone, it will most likely happen through a relationship you currently have. You might even get a referral, which is a favorable nod that it's safe and productive to do business with you.

Everything goes faster and is more productive the larger your relationship network extends. Harvey Mackay, well-known sales consultant and author of *Swim With the Sharks*, says his Rolodex is his most valuable asset. Today, we use computerized CRM-modeled programs, but the principle remains just as strong.

You can see how focus on relationships is strong. Everything we do is based on them. Every single thing is driven by relationships. In them, we experience the peaks of joy and the depths of hurt.

## FOCUS POINT

The key to understanding relationships is people. People are the most complex things on planet Earth. Your understanding of people, your self-awareness, your interpersonal skills, and your empathy play large roles in how well you can develop relationships. While every person is different, common ground for a relationship can be found if both people want to try.

## ACTION STEP

Make a list of your most valuable relationships.

When did you last speak in person with these people?

When did you last do something to show your appreciation?

Do you have a fence that needs mending with one of them?

When was the last time you asked for a referral or introduction to one of their contacts?

When was the last time you offered the same to them?

The most meaningful relationships are those that have a common bond. Treasure your relationships; your wealth is in them.

#**22**

# Respect Is the Key to Loyalty & High Performance

**I always respected my father.** We were, and still are, like night and day. He is very quiet, and only speaks when he has something essential to say. I am outspoken about my opinions and beliefs. He would rather work with animals in training, as he has been a master horse trainer for years. I prefer working with human beings in the realm of training and performance. I am not sure which is more challenging, but both are noble professions. Even though our relationship was based on entirely different viewpoints, I learned something valuable from him, which has served me well: the value of respect and where it is found.

The value of respect is found in two places: the value you place on the commitment of your word, and the value you place on other people. The opposite of these values is disrespect, which can show up through these actions:

1.  Not being on time
2.  Not learning the essentials of your job
3.  Refusing to do your best
4.  Lowering the value of leaders behind their backs with others on the team
5.  Simply not doing the right thing when the opportunity comes up

Respect for others begins with respect for yourself. As you can see from the list above, a mindset of respect is crucial for anyone who wants to achieve a level of high performance. Respect is one aspect of love, and when you feel loved and respected by another person, whether in a relationship, on a team, in a community group, or in your organization, you will go the distance. You will do what is asked and more.

## FOCUS POINT

When you respect yourself, you don't lose power or control; you gain it. The same is true with others. A lack of respect creates resistance, alienation, and resentment. Too much of this with your team can cause a revolt. I have seen it happen on more than one occasion. On the other hand, respect for others creates loyalty. Respect creates energy in followers to tackle difficult tasks and reach higher goals. When they see you respect yourself and others, they mirror this behavior as they reach higher levels of performance.

## ACTION STEP

Ask yourself some questions to know yourself better in this area:

Are you able to keep your word to yourself?

Are you able to keep your word to others?

Are you able to demonstrate respect toward others through heart-driven behaviors?

Can you leverage your respect for yourself and others to create environments of achievement and growth?

50

What behaviors do you engage in that cause you to disrespect yourself?

What behaviors do you engage in that show disrespect for others?

What changes can you start to make immediately?

# #23 BIG IDEA
## Active Listening Creates Trust & Relationships

**Distraction abounds.** In the age of constantly changing technology and rapid-fire messaging, it is extremely easy to be distracted. There are so many bright, shiny objects flying around, it's almost as if we need another label and level of distraction to lure us away from the now. The fact is that it takes a tremendous amount of energy and focus to be tethered to one thing nowadays. What's easy about reading an email, text message, or tweet is that we don't really have to pay much attention—it's more about our response than the message received. Think about it; when you see someone texting, do they take more time reading the message, or do they launch into typing?

Listening requires focus. If we really want to zero in and pay attention to what another human being is thinking and saying, it requires focus. How many of us have pretended to be listening while doing some other task? The next thing that happens is we get offended when the communicator questions our focus. We say something like, "I heard everything you said; shall I repeat it back to you?" Clue: This does not enhance relationships, as this is not a response for connectivity; it is a response for confrontation. Most of us simply do not have enough energy to focus on several things and do them well, especially listening.

Listening has levels. Level I is not listening at all, but ignoring. Not only is this not conducive to building relationships, it's rude behavior.

Level 2 is what I described in the previous section as pretend-listening. Our mind is elsewhere, and we get defensive when we are challenged to change our focus to the speaker.

Level 3 is selective listening; we just pick out the parts of the communication we think are important.

Level 4 is empathetic listening, in which our hearts are attached to the speaker, and we are moved with emotion as we are hanging on every word.

Level 5 is active listening, which is listening without judgment, but with a high degree of focus and attention.

## FOCUS POINT

To really listen to someone is the most affirmative and life-changing thing you can do. It is a vital skill to acquire. People love two things: the sound of their own name, and to feel they were heard. You can grow relationships by active listening because it shows respect and builds trust. When people do not feel listened to, they feel disrespected and unimportant; not great catalysts for trust and influence.

It starts with you.

Raise your self-awareness when you are speaking to someone else—are they really listening? If not, how are you feeling? You don't want to make others feel that way when they are communicating with you.

## ACTION STEP

Begin to actively listen. I recently asked a group of my peers and colleagues for the most effective steps we could take toward active listening.

Here is a list they helped to create:

1. Give your full attention to the other person, and focus on them.
2. It starts with presence.
3. We are actively listening when we hear the person's words, meaning, and tone.
4. We ask clarifying questions.
5. You are involved in the process; ask the right questions to uncover more about what the person is saying.
6. It's a good conversation if they are speaking 80% of the time.
7. Reflect back to their answers on key points.
8. Be aware of your own posture and word flow.
9. Practice slight and subtle mirroring of their own behaviors.
10. Care about the other person.
11. Consider your facial expression and body language.
12. Perhaps try the Listening Partnerships activity.
13. Make listening a priority! This can be applied anywhere in our world, and it should be!
14. Maintain strong, but not staring, eye contact.
15. Ask many open-ended questions, such as who, what, where, why, and how.
16. Be in the moment!
17. Disengage from technology that is present.
18. Totally remove "us" from the conversation and use the word "you".
19. Help others find answers within themselves.

20. Listen in a BIG way wider than words, and be curious about moving the conversation forward.
21. Be aware of breathing; both yours and theirs. Our breathing can be tension-filled or relaxed, so be aware.
22. Don't interrupt. Let the other person complete their full thoughts.
23. Smile (unless inappropriate for some reason). A smile is one of the most powerful expressions we can display.
24. Be overly curious to drive questions, and remain non-judgmental.

How many of these steps can you focus on in practice? Active listening is one of the easiest skills to work on, since we have several opportunities a day!

**BIG IDEA**

# Are You Listening to What Their Body Is Saying?

**Speaking without a voice.** You may have heard that 90% of our communication is non-verbal, and over 70% of that is communicated through facial expressions, gestures, etc. It's certainly true in many cases that we are using our bodies to communicate. We learn that when people are leaning in or moving closer to us, it is a positive sign, and when they are moving away, it is negative. Having long eye contact is good, and when someone is hesitant to visually engage us, it's negative. It's important to determine whether or not a person is comfortable in the current situation, as body language can mean a myriad of things. For instance, crossed arms can mean a person is not happy, or is closed off. It can also mean they are simply cold or had too much lunch.

Body language can be both a natural and a learned behavior. In the natural sense, some people's natural behavioral wiring lends itself to more facial expressions and hand gestures. Naturally extraverted individuals use these more than natural introverts. Even a small hand gesture while speaking can seem like a huge sweeping motion to the introvert. In certain situations, the ability to read people is of the utmost importance. For example, if they are really short on time and you keep them from leaving with your one more thing. Or when they are ready for you to get to the point, and you ramble on. Perhaps they really need your attention, but you don't notice and continue with your task at hand.

These are all signals for you to adjust to, and when you don't, you risk this person's future engagement with you, and at extremes, a relationship with them.

## FOCUS POINT

Wake up! If you are functioning on autopilot, and are only focusing on yourself, you enter risky territory with others. It is important to actively watch and listen to the people you want to engage. People more often say what they mean with their body language than they do with their words. You can become a more effective communicator, leader, or businessperson by observing what the other person is saying without words.

## ACTION STEP

Become a people watcher. Start watching other people in communication with each other. Watch what they do during this time with their faces, arms, legs, etc. Watch people who are really engaged with each other, and watch interactions in which one person is clearly desperate to get away. Make notes of these non-verbal cues, and then see if you can pick up on them during your own interactions.

# #25 BIG IDEA
## Dealing with Difficult People

**A difficult person and an angry person are two different things.** A difficult person is not just one who stands up for him or herself or what they believe in. We are living in a time in which people disagree, and they are automatic enemies. It doesn't have to be that way, especially if, above all else, we value people and believe their views are important, even if we do not agree with them. A difficult person could be described as simply unreasonable.

All people can be difficult at times. It takes one incident of unreasonable behavior for someone to deserve to be called difficult. Believe it or not, some folks get satisfaction from being difficult. Some enjoy engaging in an argument. Some people get joy from criticizing, and still others want to condemn and complain. For some, this is just an outward expression of conditioning they may have had over a lifetime of negative experiences. I can identify a few people who must make modifications to everything to make it "their own," simply because their lives have been without many personal victories.

No excuse can justify the stubborn and irrational behavior of a difficult person. In a perfect world, we just avoid difficult people; but in leadership, avoidance isn't possible. Leadership is about people and their issues.

## FOCUS POINT

Do your best to be a diplomat. As a leader, you can't expect to turn every difficult person around. You can only make sure that when you lay your head on the pillow every night, you are secure in knowing you have done your best. In most cases, having an exceptional attitude and being a great diplomat will not win every difficult person over. At the same time, you must realize as a leader that exceptional skills in dealing with difficult people will be of tremendous value to you in almost any position you find yourself in.

## ACTION STEP

Sit down with a pad and pen, write the name of a difficult person at the top of the page, and then list every approach or strategy you have tried as far as turning them around to be a better team member.

Have you tried to find common ground?

Have you tried to be humorous with them?

Have you tried to use a third party?

Have you probed them and asked enough questions to properly diagnose where the difficulty might be stemming from?

Remember, you need to call on all your resources and skills prior to writing them off. I promise you, the couple you turn around in your leadership career will be well worth it.

# #26

# Separate the Performance From the Person

**It is an easy trap.** We have all fallen into it and made it very personal. We have called for improvement in the person, rather than their performance. It is an area of huge improvement for those of us who coach, manage, and lead employees. I once did a session in which I asked all of the participants to list the worst coaching sessions they had been in, and the winner (or loser, depending on your perspective) said they had been told this:

"You are an idiot, completely stupid, and you have to get better right away or be fired."

"YOU" is a very personal word. I use it all the time when I am referring specifically to a person and their overall life and personal growth. However, when talking about a person's performance, the person and the performance must be separated if you want to build or maintain a person's self-esteem. Learning to separate the doer from the deed can move you forward several levels in employee development, and would not be a bad thing for all of your relationships as well.

Think deposit, not withdrawal. Dr. Covey first gave us this principle in *The 7 Habits of Highly Effective People*. The emotional bank account must have plenty of deposits, because

60

as humans, we will make plenty of withdrawals. We don't want to be emotionally bankrupt with a person. Nothing knocks a person's self-esteem down a few points like personal criticism. Kill conflict with clarity. Many cases of conflict come from varying expectations. Make sure you communicate with your employee to ensure you both have clarity on the expectations of performance. It always helps to take the personal side out of it—focus on the job, not the person. Example: "These are the objectives and tasks this position must achieve."

## FOCUS POINT

People want to be better. It is motivating to hear that your contributions are recognized and improvement is taking place. Put your focus there rather than trying to correct the mistakes you may have made in the past. As a leader, you must commit yourself to looking for the good. Change your focus to finding the gold in the person, rather than the pile of dirt you have to move to discover it. You will know you are on the right track when the employee is giving his or her own improvement measures to you, rather than vice-versa.

## ACTION STEP

Take some time to make a list. Write down some of the usual personal criticisms you have made in the past. If you are a brave person who is really dedicated to improvement in this area, ask your employees or subordinates where you have missed the boat in the past.

Make a commitment to yourself to never again engage in name-calling or labeling a person. When you are offering improvement-oriented feedback, recognize that you should always direct it toward the performance, and not the person. Practice, practice,

practice on yourself. Do you call yourself names when you make a mistake in your performance? Perhaps that is a great place to begin.

# Intentions & Impact

**I love my wife.** Since our first date, it has been my sincere intention to make her happy. I consider myself a pretty good gift giver. The secret to my success has always been to be very attentive to the people I care about. When I pick up some ideas about things they are interested in, I enjoy surprising them with some sort of gift that coincides with my observations. Ann Marie has always been a creative and aesthetic person. We had been dating for a few years, and she had mentioned a few times that she might like to learn more about photography. So, I thought for her birthday, I would surprise her with a nice camera to practice with. We had an excellent camera shop across from our offices. I visited with the owner, and picked a high-end camera. Today, she owns her own video production company!

I get so much more of a charge out of giving something than I do getting something. I just knew this was going to be a big surprise. I waited in anticipation for several weeks, but I couldn't just wait, and I started promoting the gift ahead of time. "You are just going to flip over what I have for you," I said over and over. I probably overdid that part. When the big day came, I was so thrilled. I presented the package with pride. She was immediately caught off guard at the size of the wrapped box, but I had notoriously given gifts in boxes that were designed to throw off guessing the contents. She shrugged it off, and proceeded to unwrap it. I didn't quite get the reaction I anticipated, even though I knew she was really getting into photography. I was puzzled.

The next year for her birthday, I purchased an engagement ring. It was a wonderful surprise, and after we celebrated and all the family phone calls were made, I learned something important. I learned the reason the camera wasn't that exciting—she had thought she was getting the ring the year before. This is when I learned an important lesson regarding intentions and impact.

## FOCUS POINT

We tend to evaluate ourselves on our intentions, while other people evaluate us on our impact.

Even though my intentions were the best regarding the camera, I failed to realize the impact it would have, since I totally missed the boat on what she really wanted. My intentions and impact were not aligned. Obviously, I corrected this a little while later. Perhaps if I had gotten input from some other friends, I would have known what to give her to achieve the impact I really wanted. We must look at not only our intentions, but also what impact we are going to have on other people. We need to consider all three components (intentions, impact, and input) before proceeding in order to get the impact we hope for.

## ACTION STEP

Make four columns in your journal:
- In the first column, write a person's name.
- In the second column, write your intentions regarding this person.
- In the third column, write your feedback or the device you plan to use to help them positively.
- In the fourth column, write the impact you believe this approach will have on them.

Our goal is to properly align our intentions, our tools, and the impact for the most productive and positive outcome. Unlike the scenario I described earlier, perhaps you should get others' perspectives for additional certainty of the outcome you want.

## 28

## BIG IDEA
# The Power of Agreement

**Agreements get things done.** As a matter of fact, nothing really happens without good, strong agreement. If I have the solution to your problem, it means nothing unless you're willing to agree to listen and do something about it. If you want to sell something, the point is really moot unless someone agrees to buy it from you. In the Bible, Jesus Christ said that two people making an agreement with each other is the most powerful thing they can do to accomplish something. In their popular *Boundaries* series of books, Dr. Cloud and Dr. Townsend explain how respecting rules and boundaries creates great relationships and powerful results. In other words, it's all about making and keeping agreements.

Below average leaders are afraid of agreements. Believe it or not, people fear agreements. Think about it; I'm sure you will agree. Some people will do everything in their power not to make an agreement. Everyone in my company knows if we can't get at least some form of agreement from a prospect or client about what should happen next, we can't proceed. It's a great test for relationships: which will remain versus which will fade. Certain compulsions and behaviors will prevent you from making better agreements and achieving better results. Others are just more committed to being comfortable. They refuse to make agreements that would push them higher or take them further than they are currently. They may even resent you for challenging them to go to the next level. Other people are so committed to always being right, they can't make any agreements that might put them in a position of being wrong, even if it's for mutual benefit.

## FOCUS POINT

Rules create freedom. Imagine if there were no traffic laws. If you think driving can be challenging now, what if everyone could just do as they pleased? A green or red light wouldn't mean anything. What about which side of the road to drive on, or speed? You could go seventy or you could go two mph anywhere you wanted, with no regard for anyone. You would have much less freedom and productivity without these agreements. Children and teenagers often struggle with agreements. They don't understand how keeping these agreements enhances their lives instead of inhibiting them. Adults sometimes behave this way too.

## ACTION STEP

Think about agreements. Are you confident enough to make and keep agreements with others? Are you lacking trust in yourself or others to clarify, make, and keep agreements? Or, are you somewhere in between? Think about the agreements you have made in the past and present, and think about any agreements you might make in the future that could result in great progress.

## 29

**BIG IDEA**

# Accountability Is Ownership

**A new way of thinking.** In discussions I have heard about accountability, it usually goes along the lines of leaders having to hold people accountable. This thought process follows the path of imposing accountability on people. As if you could actually produce positive results by imposing yourself on another person. What is happening is not accountability, but forced consequences. Consequences come from decisions and actions.

Leaders can only define expectations and foster accountability through example. Accountability is ownership; it's a character trait and a willingness to own your own actions and the results of those actions, good and poor. The majority of us have freedom of choice, which is the foundation of accountability. Accountability actively confronts the truth, accepts it, and embraces it. It operates brilliantly when you are willing to own your decisions and performance.

It's not always as easy as it sounds. We have been conditioned to blame external circumstances for the parts of our lives that we dislike. Sometimes we start by blaming our genetics, our environment, or maybe our parents. The blame doesn't always stop there; we blame spouses, bosses, friends, lack of resources, lack of opportunities, education, media, the economy, or maybe even our children for our flaws and failures. If we are not careful, we will give in to this conditioning to look elsewhere for the source of our shortcomings, rather than looking in the most obvious, logical, and realistic place: ourselves.

## FOCUS POINT

Accountability is the realization that you have a choice. You don't have to do anything you don't want to do. There are rewards and consequences with everything you choose to do or not to do. When you own those results based on your choices, that is real accountability. If you take the mental track that something is a have-to, it becomes a burden, and you typically meet minimum standards. When you choose to do something because you own it, you are able to tap your resources and give it your all.

## ACTION STEP

Realize that the only person who can really hold you accountable is you. When you journal on this to clarify your thinking, make sure you are being mentally honest with yourself about your circumstances and results. Remember, embracing the truth rather than being a victim is a good step in the right direction for true ownership and accountability.

# #30 BIG IDEA
## Leaders Add Value to People

**Growing leaders rarely miss an opportunity to make an impact on people.** No matter what else may be happening, they refuse to miss a teachable moment or a learning opportunity. Leaders place high value on the people they inspire, and it's a high priority to always be the best resource they can be for the people they lead. It's important to know what is needed to increase the knowledge and ability of the people who follow you. This comes from a very deep passion for helping others. Leaders get a large amount of personal gratification by helping others develop their full potential. This also creates a deep trust with followers, because they see that their leader has their best interests at heart. This includes clearing the path of potential obstacles, as well as passing on important knowledge that will increase skills.

Leaders who add value are focused on advancing others. It could be employees, family, friends, customers, or suppliers. They get a personal boost from helping someone become more valuable. That's what adding value is all about. It's taking someone you value, and making them more valuable. As a leader, your influence is never neutral. You are either adding to people, or you are subtracting from them. You are making either a deposit or a withdrawal, and all relationships work this way. Your relationships with the people around you are either growing and developing, or they are receding and dying.

In most cases, many leaders aren't mindful that this is even happening, especially when making withdrawals. Leaders are surprised when people tell them they have held them back or mismanaged the relationship.

## FOCUS POINT

As a leader who desires to add value to people, you can start by asking yourself, "How can I make things better?"

This can require you to come out of your comfort zone and be intentional about being a leader who adds value. This could be demonstrated simply by your belief in those you lead. One thing effective leaders do extremely well is believe in people, perhaps even more than they believe in themselves. My mentor, Charlie Mifflin, once told me that when I started believing in myself as much as he believed in me, the sky would be the limit. Do you think I felt valued? We can also add value with investments of time, listening, advice, and countless other methods. I have endeavored to explain why you should add value to people; you are in the best position to determine how to do that. It becomes easier once you make up your mind to do so.

## ACTION STEP

Begin to think about adding value by valuing your team of people. Valuing people is a giving opportunity. Make a list of what you have to give that would add value in a deep, meaningful way.

# #31

# Make an Effort to Understand People

**Leadership is about people and their issues.** I don't mean issues as a bad thing. We all have issues, even the best of leaders included. Leaders can have a difficult time understanding people, because it is low on the priority list. Leaders who get things accomplished through people are typically the most productive. Leaders who do not value other people and their contributions can be described as "lone wolves." They have the belief that no other person is going to measure up to themselves. They believe other people are tools to be used, rather than human beings to be respected.

This creates deep resentment amongst team members, which does not create high levels of productivity. Leaders who want to make an effort to understand people will place a greater value on others. They will want to make solid connections with the people they lead.

Since human beings will primarily act out of self-interest, it's important to look for what they value. People do have a certain level of care for their leader, but make no mistake, people are still focused on themselves. They can't help it, because they are human. Even if someone is self-sacrificing toward others, the self-sacrificing is still fulfilling a need they have. This makes understanding people particularly difficult for leaders, because most of the intentions behind observable behaviors are hidden. You can see the results, but not necessarily the causes.

Have you ever said, "Sure, go ahead and do that," when inside you were really saying, "I really wish you wouldn't do that"? This means we have to understand the things that drive people and make them tick. If we are unfocused or low on energy, we typically won't try to gain an understanding of where another person is coming from, or what is important to them.

## FOCUS POINT

Developing the ability to look at each individual, understand him or her, and make a connection is a major factor in leadership success. While not everyone will be a fit for your organization or team, having this skill will enable you to navigate the situation when things are not going to work. Understanding people will help you be compassionate and empathetic when you have to make a change.

Developing your abilities in this area will also help you in the hiring process, as many people can perform well in an interview. For example, some managers will select someone for a position because they displayed a high level of energy, only to learn later that they are scattered or unfocused. Understanding people goes deeper than just the surface level.

## ACTION STEP

Find a balance in your effort to understand people. Do not overlook weaknesses, and at the same time, do not judge too harshly. Think about how to demonstrate a sincere, caring attitude toward them, coupled with realistic expectations of the results they should be generating. In your journal, list some ways you have over- or under-emphasized the attributes of each of your team members. See if you can list some things you know are important to them, as far as self-interest is concerned. Follow up with actions you believe could counter-balance your previous approach with each of them.

**BIG IDEA #32**
## Communicating
## the Write Way

**Leaders who have developed their skill for communicating in writing can articulate their message in a clear and compelling way.** Many of the leaders I work with are very abstract in their thinking; they tend to conceptualize in bricks rather than brick walls. They rely on concrete thinkers to assemble and install the bricks where they need to be for systems and processes to be improved and implemented. This is why it is critical that leaders who tend to be more creative and abstract have the ability to communicate their ideas in a clear and written fashion. Having the aptitude to write this way makes abstract concepts, issues, and information clear and understandable.

Professional writers have the ability to bend or even break the rules of writing because they understand the rules of punctuation, grammar, and spelling. Many of us have relied on the spell check feature to help us make sure we haven't made any mistakes. Unfortunately, if the word is spelled right, spell check doesn't tell us if it is the right word. We have to go back to the basics and learn them thoroughly. Another way to increase our writing skills is to become heavy readers; not only taking in the information, but also paying close attention to the ways the author gets their ideas across effectively.

## FOCUS POINT

Place a higher importance on your written communication. Put the thought in your mind that your e-mail, letter, or text can be published publicly for all to read. As Warren Buffett said, "Are you willing to get up tomorrow morning and possibly read it in the newspaper?" Aside from the potential negative aspects, also consider whether anyone reading your communication can understand it. Look over your sentences and paragraphs to make sure it all makes sense and is clear for the reader. We know we will not reach perfection, but the higher the standard we set for our written communication, the better we will be understood, and the more we will reduce conflict and increase our positive impact.

## ACTION STEP

Good written communication takes practice. Journaling affords you a great opportunity to write outside the workplace. Imagine a year from now, someone finds your journal and begins to read your entries. Would they be able to understand how you thought and felt? Start by writing about yourself. This is a great point to begin making your communication clear. After all, who knows more about you than you? Think about a special time in your life; write about the event, and what you were thinking and feeling.

**If you conduct a survey among many leaders, it's very possible you will find a high value is placed on loyalty.** Leaders want to have the assurance that there is devotion among their followers, both to themselves and to the organization's mission. As much as we, the leaders, desire this loyalty in our followers, the instillation of loyalty begins with us. It's up to us to instill and show cause for loyalty. For instance, we must be supportive. Even though the result is reciprocity, that should not be our motivation. We should show support and loyalty to others because we are loyal. We are modeling the behavior for others to follow by showing loyalty. Equally important is preaching your loyalty practices when you have the opportunity. We are not only leaders, we are also teachers. Loyalty should be a key component in the development of the people for which we are responsible.

In my study of outstanding leaders and organizations, there is a correlation between the treatment of employees and the treatment of customers. When we show loyalty to our employees, they are more likely to show that same behavior toward customers. When we possess core values centered around treating people right, we are driven to deliver superior value to both employees and customers. Our delivery of excellent service has the tendency to create a sense of pride and purpose. This in turn draws both employees and customers in with a sense of loyalty because of the way they are treated. Our willingness to put employees' and customers' needs ahead of our own short-term goals can help build loyalty and a capacity to deliver superior results in the long-term.

## FOCUS POINT

Make sure you reward loyalty. Behavior that is rewarded is repeated. Employees who show outstanding loyalty to the organization should be shown as a standard and rewarded for their behavior; the same with customers. Care must be taken that we not reward the wrong employee or the wrong customer. When we do this, we are telegraphing a message to the rest that we want this behavior to continue. When others see behavior rewarded, whether it is acceptable or unacceptable, that is the behavior they will gravitate toward. When you, as the leader, show loyalty toward others, you become worthy of loyalty from others.

## ACTION STEP

Identify the desired behaviors you want to model for others, and others to model in turn. Make sure you reward those who demonstrate desired behaviors, and coach those that demonstrate undesirable behaviors. Create examples for each, and a game plan for how you should handle each in both employees and customers.

## BIG IDEA #34
# The Leader As a Coach

**In 1995, I listened to an audio version of a book called**
*Everyone's a Coach.* Don Shula and Ken Blanchard wrote
the book. I had been in active management for ten years at
that point. I grew up in athletics, and some of my biggest
influences were coaches. I had also been a Miami Dolphins
fan, especially during their undefeated NFL season of 1972, so
I was particularly interested in what Coach Don Shula had to
say about the methods he used to lead this amazing football
team. Believe it or not, I had never connected the coaching of
athletics to the management of people and organizations. It
was definitely a "Why didn't I think of this before?" moment.
The main points of the book were about being able to handle
quick changes or challenges, being consistent in your approach,
being honest in your dealings with people, and building trust.
These things are now staples in what I help other leaders with
today.

Coaching has become part method, part technique, and part
buzzword after I listened to that first audiobook almost twenty
years ago. The idea that not only does everyone need to have
the ability to coach, but it has almost become a necessity if
managers want to be an effective leading force for success in
an organization. For many people, the stereotype of an athletic
coach is one who gives an impassioned speech that starts
with taking no prisoners and leaving it all out on the field,
and finishes with "Win one for the Gipper!" Coaching is not
holding a one-day seminar for magic transformation, although

79

many wish this were true. Coaching is not a get-skills-quick proposition. Coaching is not just about getting results; it's about getting results for, through, and by others. You can't do a great job coaching by just believing in yourself; you must believe in the potential development of those you manage.

## FOCUS POINT

Coaching revolves around people and change. To hone your coaching skills, you need to truly care about people, in addition to being an expert on change. You are not there to coddle people. You must be able to encourage them to take charge of their own careers and take actions that maximize their potential.

Coaching revolves around a dialogue between people, not a monologue by the coach. As a coach, you must search for the keys to unlock the potential in those you manage in order to fuel their growth. Coaching can challenge your ego because as a manager, you must work to draw out what is lying dormant inside of people, rather than trying to instill something. Remember, it is always about them; it's hardly ever about you.

## ACTION STEP

Ask yourself, do you believe in people? Many managers were superstar performers because they had ultimate belief in themselves. Now that you have responsibility for other people and their success, the tables have turned. The following questions may be helpful:

Can you set aside your ego from previous success to help someone succeed tomorrow?

Do you have the patience to allow people to fail and make mistakes?

Can you allow them the space to succeed or fail, while you help them grow by being attentive and supportive?

# #35 BIG IDEA
## Squeaky Wheels Should Not Get Grease, They Should Get Replaced

**You know the saying: The squeaky wheel gets the grease.** What always amazes me about this common saying is, why would we keep greasing something that isn't working right? Why wouldn't we simply replace it with a properly operating wheel? Every team has problems and challenges. Every member of the team sees the problems and challenges. Some of them will play it safe, keep their heads down, and remain silent. This is a sin of omission—not having enough passion and caring for the organization to overcome the fear of speaking up. Unless you are in the military or in some other extenuating circumstance, it is generally not a good idea to bury your concerns. Some team members will go to the leader at the next level with a list of concerns. When this is done properly, it should be appreciated for what it is. Some of them will be complainers, and loud complainers at that. These are the squeaky wheels—the ones who believe that if they just complain at every turn, they will be heard and cause action.

What defines a squeaky wheel? What's the difference between a squeaky wheel and a team member who approaches concerns properly? Squeaky wheels complain, where others give feedback and solutions. Squeaky wheels complain about every issue without thinking it through, where others have carefully considered the issues with thorough thinking. Squeaky wheels are only concerned about themselves and how the issues affect them. Others are concerned about the organization and other team members in order to get a win-win. Squeaky wheels are defined in the leader's mind because they have considered replacing them before now. Others are defined as valuable assets who give straight feedback from the front line.

## FOCUS POINT

Pay attention to how they say it. You have heard that it's not what you say; it's how you say it. Who on your team brings up random issues out of the blue without thinking them through, and delivers them with a sarcastic tone? Squeaky wheels are painful and aggravating when you hear them. Who on your team does not know when to pick their battles? Who on your team cannot combine issues into a single problem, and it seems as if they are always bringing things up one after another?

## ACTION STEP

Identify your squeaky wheels. You must work on a succession plan for these culture killers. If you have no replacement for them, you must carefully identify the competencies needed for the squeaky wheel's position. This way, you can recruit, interview, and hire the future replacement as soon as possible. Have a discussion with your new hire regarding the behaviors that are acceptable and unacceptable while they are gaining speed to become a properly operating wheel.

# Section 3: Leading Your Organization

## BIG IDEA #36
# Great Leaders Attract the Best People

**Recruiting and hiring top talent is part of every leader's responsibility.** If you are doing things right, you will be attracting talent to your team and organization. One thing I don't see very often is what many people call "opposites attract." I don't see positive people attracting negative people, and negative people attracting positive people. It doesn't typically work that way. When it does happen, it doesn't last long. People who decide to be negative are not usually their best negative selves around positive people, and vice versa. Sometimes you have to fight this strong principle when you are drawn to hire people who are too similar to you. Organizations that understand this will put diversity training in place to try to counteract this strong inclination to hire people similar to those they already have. Birds of a feather do tend to flock together.

Great leaders look past the natural desire to recruit people who possess similar talents and processes that may already be on the team and identify what the organization actually needs most in order to win. In Phil Jackson's book, *Eleven Rings*, Jackson relates how he knew Dennis Rodman was going to be different from anyone else on the Chicago Bulls team he was coaching, and very different from any player he had in his career. Rodman was physically different. He dressed differently, wore his hair differently, and behaved differently.

He was not just different from the players on the Bulls team, but different from any other player in the NBA. This was also a positive key; he played differently. He didn't care about scoring, but he played hard and long. He played for defense and to rebound the ball. Typically coaches have to urge players to focus defensively. Not Rodman—that is where he wanted to be the best, twice winning the NBA Defensive Player of the Year Award, and being named to the NBA All-Defensive First Team seven times. Rodman and Jackson had absolutely nothing in common, but Jackson was savvy enough to get past that and find ways to bring out the best in Rodman, ultimately helping the Bulls win championships.

## FOCUS POINT

Remember, you are the guardian of the culture. Putting together a talented, diverse team of people who work together to win is no easy task. That is why multi-year championship dynasties in sports are rare. It's easier to put together a championship team than it is to keep one together. Once you have identified and selected the best people for your team, your job as a leader is just in its infancy stage. You make the transition from recruiter to leader, coach, teacher, and mentor. Each of these roles has specific approaches and skills you must develop and improve.

## ACTION STEP

Identify the talent and skills you need for your team to be the best. Do a self-analysis to identify your attributes and skills, and then determine if you need more people like yourself. Or, do you need someone else? What do your current team members need from you now while you are rounding out the team?

# BIG IDEA #37
## Understand the Impact of Change

**We all feel better in familiar situations.** We are more comfortable when the expectations are clear, and we can meet them. We are naturally less anxious and more comfortable with familiarity. This contributes to feelings of being in control, reaching a level of competency and high self-esteem. We also know that new challenges impact our organizations and workplaces. Circumstances in life do not always continue as we expect. We are forced to face new situations—sometimes with warning, sometimes with no warning.

Effective leaders know we have to change and adjust if we are to successfully adapt to the challenges the future will hurl at us. Leaders who understand the impact of change know that most people react to change with a sense of loss. This loss is of familiarity and ease of an environment to which you have grown accustomed.

There are certain terms and conditions that have been established with the people you lead. They may be written or communicated. There are also some that are assumed in the minds of the people you lead. These assumptions may not be clarified, and may perhaps go unchallenged by you for extended periods of time. They are also going unquestioned in the minds of your people. This is defined as a psychological contract between you and the people who follow you. When you change the formal or informal terms and conditions, people feel like something has been taken away. Changes that occur as "take always" can cause feelings of hurt, disappointment, or even anger.

The explicit expectations you have established are sometimes easier to deal with and modify than are the implied expectations that exist in the heads of your people. Unlike the explicit expectations that are verbalized or in writing, the implied ones are taken for granted, since they have never been stated.

## FOCUS POINT

Your role as an effective leader is not to protect people from change. You must help them adapt to change. Change is going to happen, and is a reasonable response to the shifting world we live and work in. Your role is to be highly aware of the impact change will have on the people you lead. You must strategize and plan in order to make acclimation to change happen more smoothly. You must learn to address issues openly, and treat people with proper respect by allowing dialogue with you—this will help your team work through the transition from old business to new business.

Your quality employees will have a greater willingness to adapt to the changes and move on. Others may be less adaptable, which may provide insight into their future with your company. The main point is to approach the change with a respectful, fair, and honest attempt to help make the transition.

## ACTION STEP

Consider the changes you are thinking about making. Are they explicit and acknowledged, or are they implicit assumptions? You have to recognize your people's need for support in a new situation. Be open and honest about your expectations—both those that are explicit, and those that have been assumed. Bring them out into the open, and clarify the boundaries. Make sure you support your team members' self-esteem with acknowledged interest and value for people.

# #38 BIG IDEA
## Planning Is More Valuable Than Plans

**All leaders and organizations need a plan.** Plans keep us from drifting day to day. They force us to clarify our assumptions and our thoughts about the future. They help us become proactive rather than reactive, and they put us in a position to deal with explosive growth and/or massive decline. Effective planning is a huge challenge because you must deal with lack of control of the future, lack of certainty about conditions that are always subject to change, and inconsistency of people in their approaches and responses. You also cannot afford to spend too much time in the planning process, as it can become a never-ending project.

In the process of planning, you must realize that all assumptions are dangerous—especially the assumption that your plan will be absolutely successful. You shouldn't presume every aspect of your plan is going to go as you hoped. It's probably more effective to assume your plan might explode. Don't get me wrong, I am a total proponent of staying relentlessly positive. At the same time, realize that when you are pulling together a variety of internal/external conditions, circumstances, and groups of people, one or more of them is very possibly going to go awry. It is virtually impossible to fully predict how a decision or a plan will turn out.

## FOCUS POINT

Planning is the most beneficial part of a plan. The process of planning causes you to explore many options and objectives. However, it is not an exact science or a perfected art. It is a balance of experience, insight, conceptual and futuristic thinking, and problem solving. The most successful leaders consider as many uncontrollable realities and uncertainties as possible. The fact that there is no guarantee your plan will be successful is very real. You will need to stay as engaged as possible to ensure its successful completion. Plans seem to take on a life of their own as they are implemented.

## ACTION STEP

In regards to your plans, how flexible, open-minded, and observant are you? Take each of these skills, and note any improvement areas you need to enhance. Get feedback from those who execute your plans. These are huge keys to success. As conditions change, so should your skills.

# #39 BIG IDEA
## Building the Customer Mindset

**Peter Drucker said that the purpose of a business is to create, service, and keep a customer.** We have seen plenty of customer service mantras and clichés. The customer is number one, and the customer is king. "You only have one boss," Sam Walton said, "and that is the customer." The key to delivering exceptional customer service is not to instill a bunch of rules. It's not the rules that will make you effective, it is a customer-oriented mindset that will drive you to ensure the customer is satisfied and valued. Organizations that deliver outstanding customer service are driven by a genuine desire to satisfy the customer. This desire is built on the idea that everyone is a customer: the people who buy your product or service, your owners, and your employees—everyone is a customer of yours.

A mindset set of higher-level customer service cannot be based only on satisfaction. Satisfaction is the lower end of the standard. If people are satisfied with your company, they are just lukewarm about what you are doing for them. If your customers are simply satisfied, they really don't have a compelling reason to stay with you, and could possibly leave for another company that provides more than satisfaction. The question is: How do you create raving fans of your product or service? The most effective way is to constantly create conversations with them. Ask them questions and build rapport. The benefit of building these relationships is very valuable, and will pay you dividends in the future. The customer values this connection, and you and your staff will increase your customer knowledge and build experiences with them.

## FOCUS POINT

Insure yourself against mistakes. When it comes to serving customers, any problem is an opportunity. This is a chance to really show how much you value them by shifting the customer mindset. Often we attribute disempowerment to a faux pas that has occurred with a customer. On the other hand, if we build strong relationships with our customers, how we resolve the problem and take care of them can make the relationship even stronger and more secure. The main thing to remember is to not get defensive; don't pass it off or blame someone else. Take action immediately with a couple of options designed to create value on behalf of your customer and solve the immediate problem. If you can go above and beyond the immediate problem without giving away the store, you can do the most valuable thing possible: leave the customer with a positive story rather than a negative story to tell.

## ACTION STEP

Think about your current customer mindset. What are your values and policies concerning customers? Do you have a way to solve customer problems that leaves them happy, rather than disgruntled? What story do you have them telling after dealing with your company on a mistake?

# #40 BIG IDEA
## The Reality of the Marketplace

**Where results happen.** In business, the marketplace is where results take place. It's where performance is truly evaluated while qualifications are authenticated. Growing up in Kentucky on a farm, we were always talking about "going to market." The market was where we would get paid for our livestock and grains. Our key objective was to get our animals and produce "to market," because the measurement of success or failure for that year was based on the results we achieved at the market. Of course, in that situation, we were referring to the market as a specific geographic destination where we would be transporting our product. Today, the marketplace is everywhere and all the time. It exists everywhere and nowhere. It is millions of buying and selling decisions taking place daily, in all areas of the world and at all levels—from one penny to trillions of dollars. It is the place where results take place.

In the marketplace, much of its operation centers on how much of something exists coupled with how many people want it, and to what degree they want it. These forces determine the pricing of products in the marketplace. Typically, this pricing is the result of information on the product—both now, and also speculatively in future times. When these factors are allowed to naturally ebb and flow without any outside interference (government or otherwise), this is known as a free market.

Generally speaking, the freer the market, the more vibrant the opportunity in the marketplace.

This has been shown to create more wealth and opportunity for more people. In the marketplace, the opportunity of a lifetime exists only during the lifetime of the opportunity. Much of a leader's job is to accurately make decisions regarding the marketplace.

## FOCUS POINT

The economic qualifications of a leader are determined in the marketplace. Leadership success in business is not limited to people skills. It is also a result of your ability to enter the market with products and services you can sell in a competitive environment. If you are fortunate enough to live in a free market, you are enabled to start with an idea.

Combine that with energy and passion, and you have the opportunity to enter the marketplace with a business. You may not be an entrepreneur, but you may be tasked with the management of a business or an organization. You are tasked with the same mission: you must make decisions for the long-term health, survival, and success of that organization in the marketplace.

Leaders sometimes come under heavy criticism for only thinking about profits. We need to realize that while caring about the employees and customers of the enterprise is critical, so too is being a steward of the company's well-being, which is directly tied to success in the marketplace.

## ACTION STEP

Identify your company's success factors in the marketplace. Determine your costs to buy, make, or sell something. Determine what the marketplace is willing to pay for your product or service. What are the short- and long-term results you are setting as goals? What results would show you are doing a bad job or a good job as leader?

## BIG IDEA #41
# The Importance of Stories

**Your life is a story.** In my experience of working with executives, there are times they tend to randomly remember the best and worst of situations in their lives. These memories are stories that have not been thought about in years, and are residing in their subconscious influencing their current actions. These embedded life experiences are possibly shaping values and beliefs, because every human being has been immersed in the stories of their own lives, both of their own making and those told them by others. The randomness of these thoughts can be interruptive. To retrieve some of those stories, to help pull them to the conscious from the subconscious, I assign an exercise of writing down a sequential group of numbers that correspond with their ages for every decade they have lived. Number One equals ages one through ten years old. Two equals eleven through twenty years old, and so on, to the current day. Then I ask them to write the highlights of their lives for each decade. Once completed, they see the panoramic highlights and threads of the story of their lives.

Branding is storytelling. What these executives begin to realize is that their story makes up a large part of their personal brand. Personal brands and corporate brands are powerful in correlation with the stories behind them. No matter what media you use, it is just a medium to tell a story. When this is done correctly, the impact is very powerful because of the way this works on a larger scale. Human beings have a tribal mentality, and like to feel part of a narrative that is bigger. We look for stories to define who we are, what we are about, and where we belong. This is where true company pride comes from. It's why your employees want to wear apparel that features your company logo and image. It bonds them and displays them as part of the larger image and narrative. The stronger you make the story, the more they want to be a part of it. It works the same way with affiliated entities. When you have an Apple computer, that story and image helps define you. The same happens when you drive a Chevy, BMW, or Mercedes, or when you wear Nike or Under Armour.

## FOCUS POINT

Leaders use stories. If you look throughout history, you will find that most notable leaders have utilized powerful stories to attract and maintain followers. When you use stories to strengthen corporate business brands, they can come in the form of myths, legends, traditions, rules, codes, and even laws. These things also create the corporate culture, which adds fuel to the overall corporate narrative and the corporate brand. Leaders use stories because stories are emotional—they help illustrate, and they can create powerful affiliations. Why are movies so popular? People love stories because they accomplish a critical function for our thinking. They help us make sense of our lives, and help us explain things to ourselves.

## ACTION STEP

Outline your company story:

How did it start? Use my decade formula to chart the history of the company, writing the highlights.

Then, try to do the next ten to twenty years, and project where the story is going.

Now make a list of how you are going to tell the three parts of the company story.

# #42 BIG IDEA
## Getting Alignment in Your Organization

**Is alignment an afterthought?** Organizations spend quite a few hours on strategic planning. Getting the right plan is definitely important, and organizations spend hours on structure. Having the right structure to follow your strategy is definitely important. The thing that seems interesting is the lack of time spent on gaining alignment. This is why important goals, metrics, and targets get knocked off track somewhere in the process of implementing the plan. One of the most common reasons the strategic plan gets off track is because of failure to recognize the cross-functional nature of most strategies and goals. Departments have to work together. If the sales department has a strategy to sell 1,000 truckloads of widgets, but manufacturing can only produce 500 truckloads, then that particular goal will not be met no matter how brilliant the strategy is. Clearly, the alignment of outcomes is missing from this scenario. This is not at all uncommon in organizational structure today.

Achievement of alignment across an organization means clarity of communication. It is important to allow participation and have transparency of the strategy and the goals of all departments. This can reduce redundancy of the work effort and redundancy of goals; it can also reduce conflicts. Sharing of this process allows managers and employees to find better ways to support each other. It also helps identify areas where they might actually be working at cross-purposes with other departments. You also have to remember, prior to this kind of cross-functional goal process, every department needs to be in alignment with your corporate core ideology. Having alignment with the purpose, vision, and core values of the organization is a strict non-negotiable item which cannot be ignored prior to setting cross-functional strategic plans and goals.

## FOCUS POINT

What is the overall goal? Knowing the overall goal for the organization is critical to setting a strategic plan. Once you have that, then you can do what you need to do in order to align with it. Much of organizational alignment is about values. That doesn't mean you don't get a voice about how things are being done, but it does mean the work you and the organization are doing is meaningful to you. There are guidelines to how we treat each other and how we interact as we plan how to reach goals together. If you don't have this in place, you have individual managers playing their own songs, rather than participating in the organizational symphonic opus.

## ACTION STEPS

Think about how you can help to align your organization. Alignment is all about values, communication, and agreement. Which of the three are you missing? Which ones need clarification and/or focus? What can you do right now with the help of your team to gain better alignment in your organization? Write them down.

## BIG IDEA
## Not Understanding Risk
## Is Risky Business

**It's interesting how people perceive risk.** Some people will not get anywhere near the stock market. Years of market ups and downs combined with powerful images of the Great Depression cause people to think of the market as a risky place. Some people will flock to casinos and gambling boats. In the case of casinos, you typically hear fantastic stories about the one big winner, and nothing about the hundreds of thousands of losers. In the case of the market, you typically hear about the one big loser, and nothing about the thousands of winners. In each case, there are degrees of risk involved, as there are in almost every aspect of life. Those who understand the risks in each scenario, and navigate the risks successfully usually come out on top.

Maslow nailed it. Abraham Maslow, in his "hierarchy of needs" theory, said safety and security were our most powerful needs. These needs trump greatness and seeing ourselves as our greatest selves. This tells us we avoid risk generally to protect our level of security. Only in the case of negative peer pressure, clever advertising, or social trends do we totally ignore this principle. The reason these things are successful in getting past our safety and security needs is: we do not see the negative risks until the damage is done and it is too late.

How many of us would not smoke, or put too much money on our credit cards, if the risks were more apparent and visible? We don't try to jump the Grand Canyon with our bicycle because the risks are pretty apparent and visible.

## FOCUS POINT

No risk, no reward. The avoidance of risk is a major limiting factor in a person's success. The key is not avoiding risk altogether, but approaching it with careful thought and preparation. This is known as a calculated risk. Learning to calculate risk to reduce failure and increase success is one of the most important things a leader can do. Not doing this in a leadership position is as reckless as some of the aforementioned items. If you consider yourself a risk-taker, hopefully you calculate your risks to bring yourself closer to your success goals. If not, perhaps you should consider taking a step back to re-examine how you approach risk.

## ACTION STEP

Learn all you can about the risk involved. Mitigating risk has to do with understanding the rules and scope of the risk you are taking. Good research and verified data help you be a better risk manager. Good information allows you to walk away from situations that are too risky, and gives you the peace of mind that you avoided a big mistake. On the other hand, building this confidence will also make you a better risk-taker and put you in a position to navigate the risk and come out the winner.

Also, keep in mind that the best scenario is one in which you have also protected your downside by not putting all your eggs in one basket in order to avoid a complete loss, in case things don't work out as you had planned. It is a huge confidence boost when you put yourself in a position to be fine no matter how the risk turns out.

## BIG IDEA #44
# Take a Three-Dimensional Look at Your People

**It's not a secret.** When it comes to exceptional product and customer service, the companies that immediately come to mind include The Ritz-Carlton, Nike, and Amazon. How do these companies continuously grow their businesses through amazing customer service? The leadership of these companies understands that it starts with getting talented people, and then investing in the process of developing them to their larger potential.

It's not luck. Shortsighted companies invest minimally in developing their people, and when they do, they think in terms of hard training skills such as software training. Soft skills, which create engagement, are often overlooked. Also, when things get tight, the first thing companies cut is the training budget. What kind of message do you think that sends to the people? Big-time success in business does not come from luck. It comes from energizing the leverage where you have the most investment. Your people want their talents applied and their contributions recognized.

### FOCUS POINT

Spend time thinking about what your people do to help your business succeed. What could you do to further enhance and develop their potential? Look position by position and person

107

by person. Look at their strengths for ways to help, not their weaknesses. How can you enhance them and make them even stronger? It might be leadership, time management, strategic thinking, execution, or a dozen other areas you could focus on to boost their productivity and give them the impression you really care about their success. Their success equals your success.

## ACTION STEP

Your company will not get to greatness by chance. You will get there by focusing on being effective at the right things. Your assignment is to put on your 3-D glasses and focus on your people. Here's how:

1. Determine your people: Evaluate them. Determine what the job requires of them, and then determine where they are in relation to that. Is it a skills gap or a coaching gap?
2. Develop your people: Grow them and help them. Once you have determined why and where, set about helping what and how.
3. Deploy your people: Put them in the game. Allow them to put their talents to work for your customers and company. Evaluate often, coach when necessary, praise liberally.

Don't forget that the true potential growth of your business comes in and out of your doors every day and night. Happy, empowered, and engaged people equal the same behaviors in your customers.

# Brands Are Sorting Devices

**The use of brands is everywhere in advertising and marketing.** It's very difficult to go anywhere and not be affected by brands, no matter how hard you try to avoid their influence. You drive down the highway, and they are there, you open a cabinet in your kitchen, they are there, you go to a movie, they are there, you turn on the television, well, you get the idea. I've seen research that shows that during an average day, an average consumer has contact with about 1,700 various branded products.

Brands are not just product- or corporate-based. You come in contact with what we would call corporate brands of businesses and organizations, but you also come in contact with personal people brands. Brands can be product and also people-focused.

**Product- and company-focused:**
*Apple, Bank of America, Wal-Mart*

**People-focused:**
*Oprah Winfrey, Richard Branson, Guy Kawasaki*

Brands are sorting devices. Brands help identify and amplify both the desire to do business and the experience of doing business with your company. Your brand is either increasing or decreasing your chances of being selected.

## FOCUS POINT

Evaluate the satisfaction of your personal results as well as your organization's results. Do you think dissatisfaction could be caused by a lack of clear brand definition, or perhaps brand weakness? Having a successful brand does not come by accident. Most successful companies and people do not leave their image and brand to chance. They are not sending mixed messages to the target audience. A powerful brand differentiates you from your competitors, and projects a powerful promise you must work hard to fulfill. People will always pay more for a product or service that consistently delivers what is promised.

## ACTION STEP

Ask yourself:

What would your brand be worth?

Are you always building equity?

Is what you represent what you actually deliver?

Do you deliver an amazing experience along with what you promised?

BIG IDEA #
# Responsibility to Employees #**46**

**One of the attributes of a strong leader is responsibility.**
In my practice of working with leaders and their companies,
my definition of a responsible leader is anyone with the ability
to respond proactively to support the team. It includes the
people who touch a particular process or issue; but can
this support go too far? Yes, it can. As a leader, you accept
responsibility for employee output, productivity, and results.
You are responsible to help in these areas by giving people
the tools and training needed to do their jobs. This is part of
your responsibility to them. At the same time, you are not
responsible for them. Continually rescuing employees from
things they should be learning and doing on their own keeps
them dependent on you. This is being responsible for them,
not to them.

All people have value. People are not computers; they don't
always do the right thing. They are fallible and susceptible to
the same flaws as the leader. You have a responsibility to them
to value them as human beings. Your responsibility impels you
to do your best in this area, but at the end of the day, you
cannot do their jobs for them. I have seen many Superman
leaders. An employee begins to struggle, and the leader ducks
into the nearest phone booth, changes into their super leader
costume, then rushes in at the last minute to save the day.
Sheltering and rescuing a person from natural consequences
teaches and reinforces irresponsibility.

## FOCUS POINT

Everything you do sends a signal. Make sure the signals you are sending are congruent and consistent. Being responsible for themselves and their results is an absolute requirement if employees are to truly succeed in their department or organization. Whatever you accept becomes the standard of performance. If you are inconsistent, this sends a message to your employees that the rules and exceptions are variable, depending upon who you are or perhaps your relationship to the leader. This is a recipe for confusion and variance in performance across the board.

## ACTION STEP

Create a responsibility list. Have you been responsible to or for your people? Make a two-column list. In one column, write the things you think you should do or provide in order to be a responsible leader to your people. In the second column, write a list of things they are responsible for doing, and the results they are supposed to be generating. Once you have completed your lists, sit down and go over them for each person on your team to ensure clarity and communication. Consistently refer back to this list whenever the opportunity arises.

**Momentum is a powerful thing.** Momentum can sometimes determine your fate with an organization, a project, or an elusive goal you set. Momentum is generally described as "the force of movement," and momentum is fairly evident when you sense that nothing can stand in your way—mistakes seem to be minimized, and change is not so hard. The domino theory is in full effect, and one falls right after another. Conversely, if momentum is swinging against you, it feels like all your wheels are buried in three feet of heavy mud, and all action results in no movement at all.

Recognizing the movement of momentum is key. It is important to recognize when you are going with the wind, and when the wind is blowing straight against your face. We teach about resistance with the axiom: "Whatever you resist, persists." It's very much like sinking and fighting in quicksand. The more movement you make, the faster you sink. Once you recognize the direction of your momentum, you can take appropriate action.

If the momentum is with you, push. In the military, there is an interesting principle that helps you reinforce when you are winning. If you break through an enemy's position, that is when you send in reserves to deepen the penetration of your force. If you have momentum on your side in your business or on a project, keep pushing forward and do not stop. Let one success build on top of the next, and let the momentum accelerate and intensify. This is when your mind will send you signals telling you it's time to slow down or take a break. While you do want to enjoy your success or celebrate, you do not want to stop the momentum. If the momentum is against you, release. I know this is counter-intuitive. When things are not going well, it is easy to get caught up in the counter-momentum. In sports, this is generally when coaches call time-outs. They know the more they fight against the opposing momentum, the more the momentum will work against them, so they take a break. Did you ever notice how thirty or sixty seconds can make a huge difference? This time allows for settling of the emotions, regaining mental clarity, and resetting of energy. It is interesting that when people are losing against momentum, they whip themselves to work harder.

## FOCUS POINT

Know the direction of the momentum in your life or business. When the momentum is with you, it takes less energy to push the momentum along. When the momentum is against you, it will drain you of all your energy with very little result for your effort. No matter how you press, it will be like the dream you have in which your running results in hardly any movement. Isn't that frustrating? I hate that dream. A savvy leader who is engaged instantly knows which way the momentum is moving. This leader knows how to control it, and which buttons to push to be effective. It seems counter-intuitive to let everyone off work early to celebrate when it seems you aren't doing well, but it does work. A good leader knows how to take control of whatever pressure exists.

## ACTION STEP

Take a moment to think of where you are pushing yourself hard and getting little return.

Are you working more hours at work, but making little or no more money?

How can you take a break to renew your mental clarity and energy?

Take a moment and think of where you are moving forward rapidly. Are you on a roll where it seems like everything is falling into place for you with very little effort?

How can you push yourself even more in that area?

# #48 BIG IDEA
## Decisions Are Like
## a Batting Average

**Getting in the Hall Of Fame.** I have a leadership maxim that I have used as an example to leaders I have coached since mid-1980: You only have to be successful in your decisions slightly more than 30% to be voted into the Baseball Hall of Fame. Hitters in professional baseball must make a decision on each pitch. This poses the question: To swing or not to swing? When a hitter delivers a safely hit ball on three out of every ten pitches, they are considered among the game's greatest decision makers and execution specialists.

Decisions are a percentage, too. I have long believed (and have seen some research to back it up) that, like hitting in baseball, 70% of our decisions are going to turn out wrong, and 30% of our decisions are going to be the correct ones. If you think about it, how many decisions do you make in one single day? Hundreds. For example: what to wear, what to say, what to do, where to eat, etc. If we could manage to land the big, impactful decisions inside that 30% range, we would be doing very well. We could then allow those small, inconsequential decisions to land within the 70% range.

I am convinced that many decisions are based on little regard for the future. For many leaders, the present moment is all that is considered. Leaders that tend to live for today are usually disappointed with the results of tomorrow. Principled, vision-oriented leaders are very focused on what is right and wrong for the long-term vitality of the organization. They believe strongly in their core ideologies, and they allow these to guide the decision-making process.

## FOCUS POINT

Think about your batting average. If we had a score card on the decisions you have made this year, how would your score look? What would your average be? Since the mid-80s, I have made it a practice to record every major decision I made during the course of a year, along with its results. I record the results for that particular year, and also over time. This includes major initiatives I decided to launch, hires I decided to make, and major purchases I made. Over time, I have found I usually make between thirty to thirty-five major decisions per year.

## ACTION STEP

Make your list.

How many major decisions are you making this year?
(If possible, list the ones from last year and the results also.)

How many of these have you made so far?

How many are going well, and how many are failing?

What have you learned from both the successful ones and the ones that are less successful?

# #49 BIG IDEA
# Leaders Measure Results

**Measurement. Where would we be if we didn't measure results?** Think about it. At the end of the day, how will you know if you are successful without measurement? Measurement can sometimes sound scary. We might think it is overly complicated, or perhaps that it will be costly to measure. Measuring results is a reality check, and most of the time, it takes all feeling and emotion out of the process, painting a more realistic view of your performance. This may be part of the problem, because sometimes we will protest and say whatever we can to get away from our own performance. Leaders must own their performance, and measurement helps tell the true score.

The sooner we can acknowledge the truth about our performance, the faster we can adjust and accelerate. Denial or not knowing is where we get stuck. Effective measurement demands our attention and creates a system to respond more quickly, increasing our chances of success in the future. It allows us to look back, and gives us projections on looking forward. Most organizations do a good job of measuring past performance such as sales, cash flow, pounds lost, etc.

Sometimes there is a lack of measuring the most important result, which would give you a projection of your future result. The reality is, you have greater control over your present actions and execution than you do over your results. Your actions create your results and give you power over your day.

## FOCUS POINT

Creating a way to measure your results is essential, because it gives you a map of where you have been and where you are going. If you can design a system that measures your execution, you can pinpoint breakdowns and make changes. It may take some time before you can get a feel for your past results, but measuring your execution can happen every day, and that is the only place where your true action-taking power lies. In this way, if you are executing at a very high level, but the results are not showing up, you may need to go back and adjust the plan. For every action, there is a reaction—when you execute, you are producing something. Measurement allows you to see if that is the something you intended.

## ACTION STEP

Measure your execution by working from a plan. This way, you can evaluate how successfully you are executing. Once you set up your plan for executing, and you begin evaluating your results, focus on excellence rather than perfection. Excellence is achieved by increasing your execution and moving toward your optimum measurement. Your focus needs to be on getting better every day, creating the intention to always surpass your previous best.

# #50 BIG IDEA
## Simplifying Strategy

**Killing the complexity.** After years of helping companies define and create strategy, one thing I have learned is that often they are struggling with complexity. There are too many opportunities, ideas, and explanations. E.F. Schumacher explained it this way: "Any intelligent fool can make things bigger, more complex, and more violent. It takes a touch of genius— and a lot of courage to move in the opposite direction." Focus comes from elimination, not by adding things on. Some famous examples include, "Pizza delivered in 30 minutes or less, or it's free," from Domino's. Or even more simple is from Southwest Airlines: "Wheels up." Southwest knows that if that hunk of metal is in the air more than their competition, they are going to make more money.

Make it as simple as possible. One way to do this is to boil it down to one powerful phrase. Having a simple, powerful, one-phrase strategy provides not only clarity in the marketplace, but also clarity within your organization. You need to ensure that your one-phrase strategy is not just a set of words you use, but that it provides substance to your strategy. This requires developing a set of actions that will identify what you do differently, which will provide credibility to your one-phrase strategy. Ask yourself and your team this question: What key actions do we do to support our one-phrase strategy? Remember, the one phrase you select forms the basis and core of your strategy, but it also forms the focus of the activities that support it. In the case of the phrase Southwest uses, it means no advance reservations for seating, and using the same aircraft model across all their fleet— just a few of the key activities supporting "Wheels Up."

## FOCUS POINT

Strategy can be very complicated, but winners make it simple. This weekend, I was reading a book about how Alan Mulally engineered the great turnaround of the Ford Motor Company. When he arrived, the brands were Ford, Lincoln, Mercury, Land Rover, Jaguar, Aston Martin, Volvo, and Mazda. The brand that was suffering the most was the brand named after its founder—Ford. In order to save the iconic company, Mulally believed they had to focus on and invest in one brand: Ford. His one-phrase strategy was, "One team, one plan, one goal." Clarity is power, and is the key to communicating while having a healthy organization. You can immediately see the impact that having a simple one-phrase strategy can provide your organization.

## ACTION STEP

Find the common language. Begin working to find the language you can use with your team to describe your strategy in its simplest form. You need a small, simple vision, and gigantic, massive alignment around it.

# Section 4: Leading Your Community

## BIG IDEA #51
## Giving Is Power

**Service: There is a lot of talk about servant leadership.** Service is about giving—giving of yourself, giving of your gifts and talent, and giving from your abundance of whatever you have to give. The average leader lives an ordinary life with a singular focus on the immediate things around. The exceptional leader lives an extraordinary life, and chooses to make great contributions to community, company, family, and customers. Exceptional leaders also give to those they may never meet. Their giving impacts on a larger scale, and makes a huge difference in the lives of people. Simply, these leaders make giving a big part of living. No matter where they are, these leaders are always looking for ways they can contribute.

Giving isn't just money. Typically when people think of giving, they think of money. However, there are a lot of ways a person can give of himself or herself besides money. Of course, money is a powerful tool, and everyone needs it for economic exchange purposes. I am not downplaying it; money is important. But, if you limit everyone's contribution to money, you are going to really limit the power of giving. The average leader just wants to survive. They just want to get by. The exceptional leader gives to themselves and to others. They find great balance in their giving.

Being generous with yourself increases your capacity to help other people. Giving equals power. When you find the ability to balance giving to yourself, not excluding giving to others, but including others, you have found a powerful giving lifestyle.

## FOCUS POINT

Find the balance. If you were to give everything away—all your talents and money—it wouldn't be long before you would be completely drained and have nothing. If you were to save everything—all your talents and money—it wouldn't be long until nothing would be working for you, and you would develop a mindset of hoarding. If you don't spend time to take care of yourself, you won't have a life to give. You need to give yourself and your resources; this develops appropriate self-worth and self-esteem. In this way, you are appreciative of the value and blessings you have, and what they can do for others. This is how giving gives you power.

## ACTION STEP

List the ways you are building and taking care of yourself, then list the ways you are giving of yourself and your resources, and make a note of who it is helping. Leaders demonstrate their power not by how much they accumulate, but by how much they give.